A301. 35

the Art of Watercolour

by Charles Evans

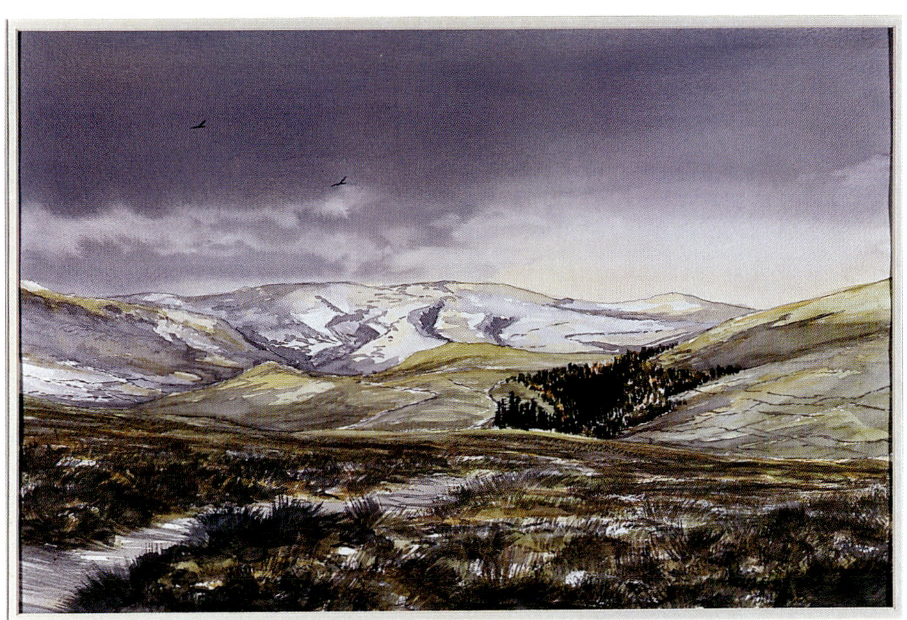

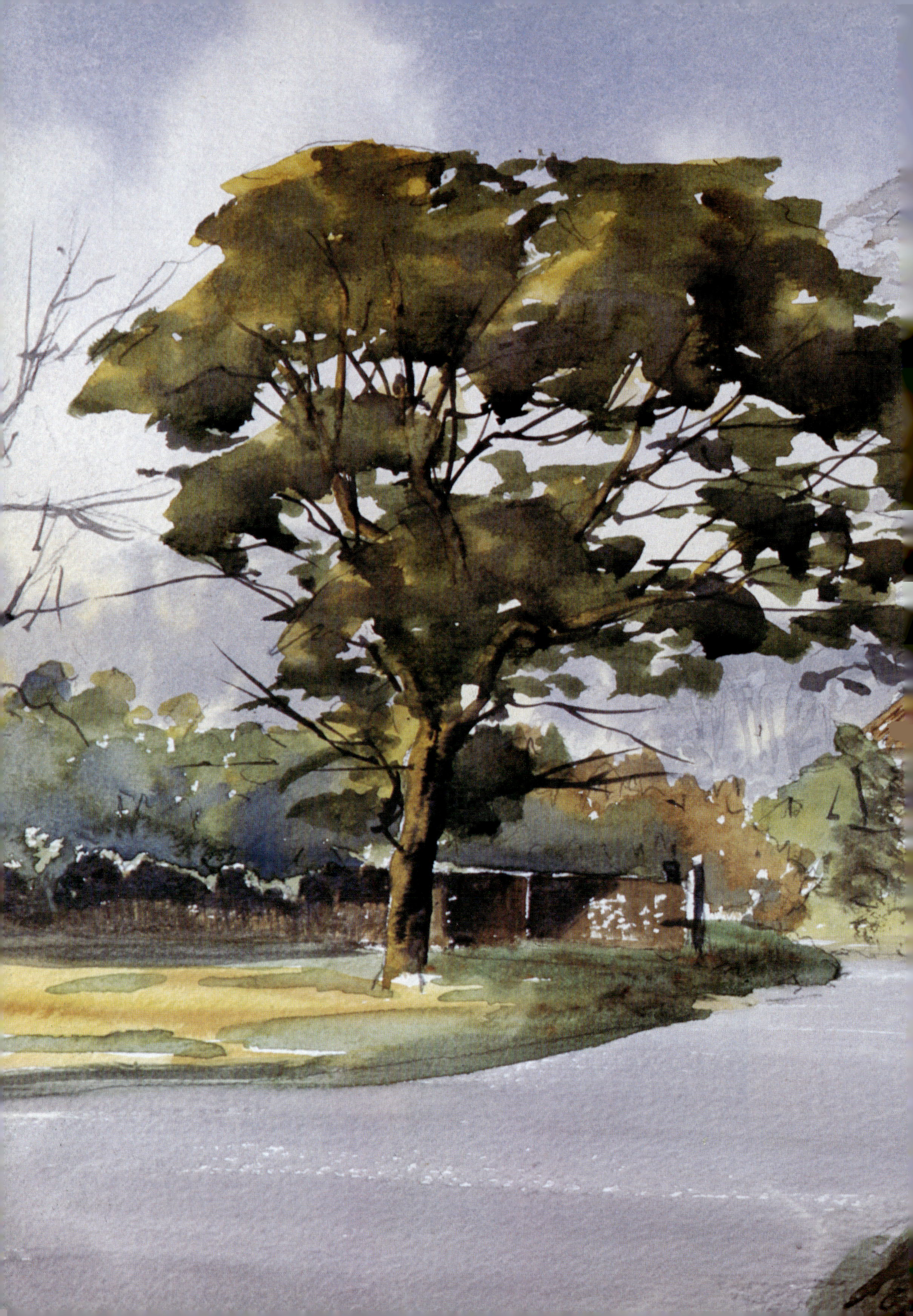

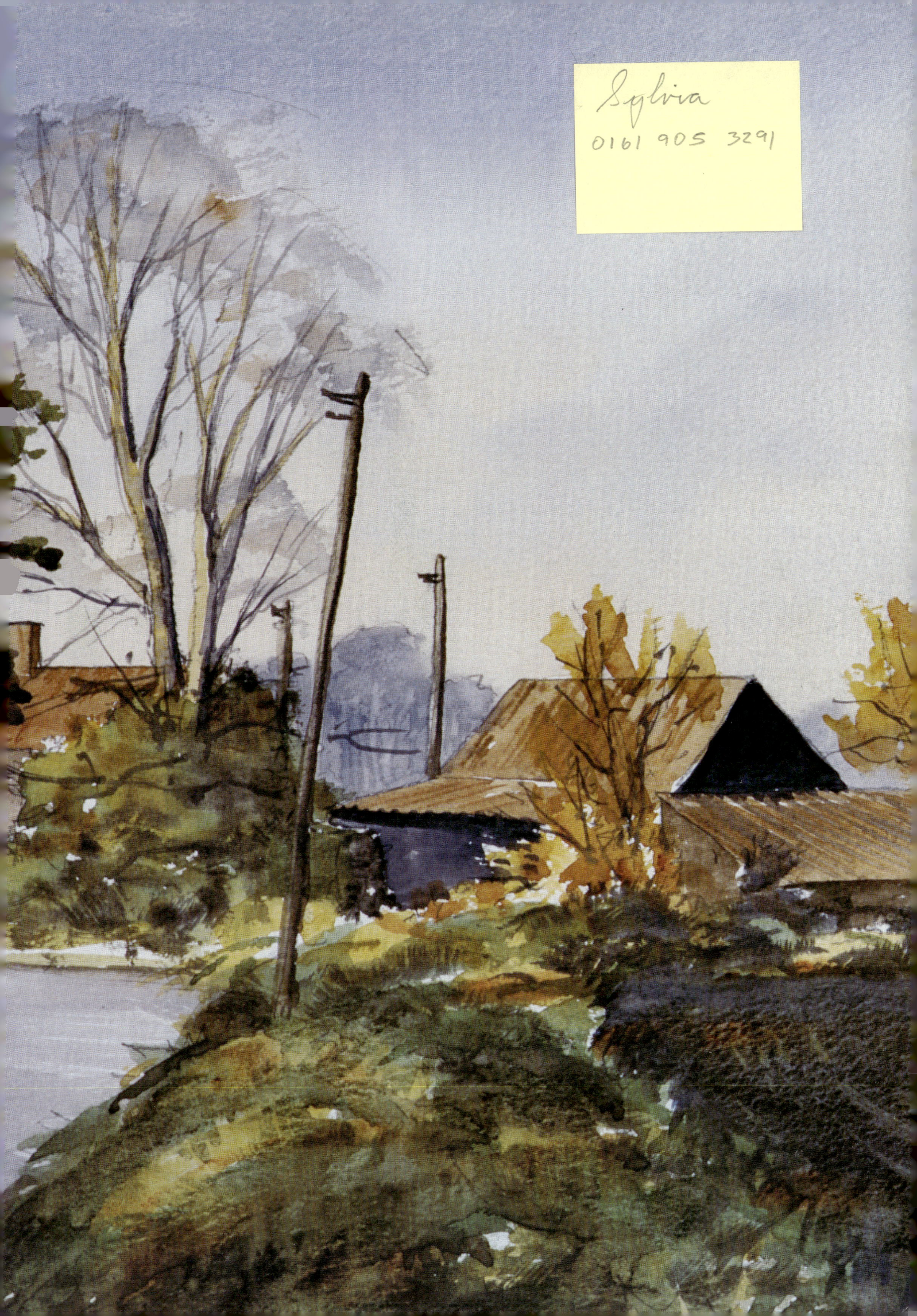

Foreword

I FIRST met Charles Evans painting Alnwick Moor on a typical Northumbrian summer's day. It was lashing with rain, it was blowing a gale, and even the sheep were complaining. I don't know who was acting the most strangely. Charles, in that he was attempting to paint watercolour with a muddy stream running into his boots and a torrent running off his nose and down onto the foreground. Or me, who was trying to film him doing all of this. Since then we've had lots of fun, painting and filming in snow, wind and rain, in boats and hanging off helicopters, and sometimes even in nice warm dry conditions where the light and the scene are just so. Wherever we are, Charles always paints so well, and can communicate his love of painting and his skill with a brush in a way that is both enthusiastic and infectious. If you learn anything from this man, it should be to throw yourself into every scene you paint. Good advice, unless you happen to be in a very muddy field, in a hailstorm, and with a TV crew recording your every move for posterity.

MARK MURRAY
Producer, TTTV

First published in Great Britain 2000

Publishing and Copyright 2000 by:

Ward Philipson Group Ltd.,

Halifax Road, Dunston Industrial Estate,

Gateshead, Tyne & Wear NE11 9HW.

Tel: (0191) 460 5915

Fax: (0191) 460 8540

e-mail: charlesevans@theartistshop.co.uk

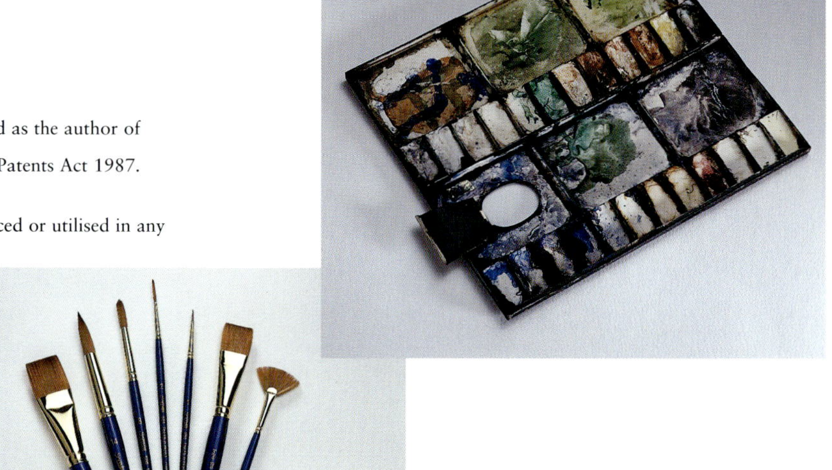

Photography, Design,
Reproduction and Printing by:

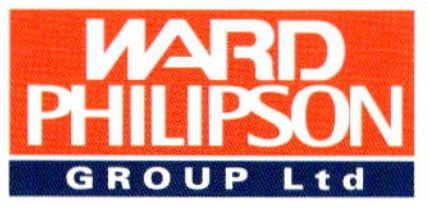

Tel: (0191) 460 5915

I.S.B.N. 0 9534224 2 9

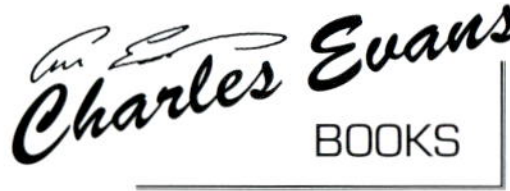

Contents

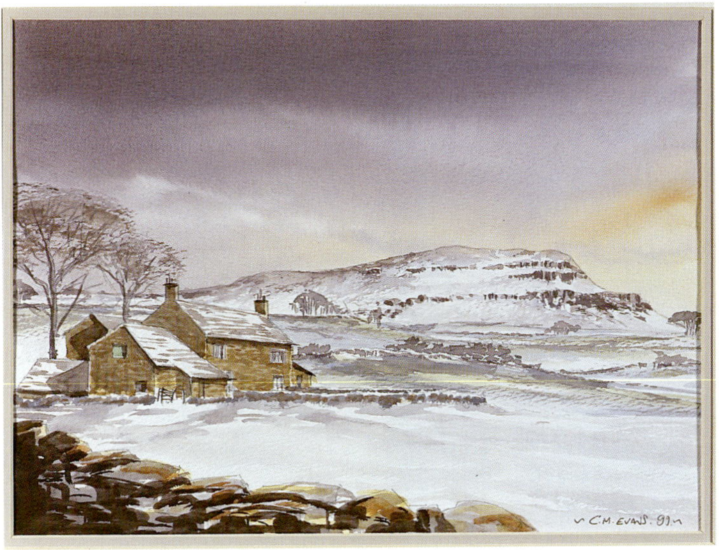

Portrait of the Artist

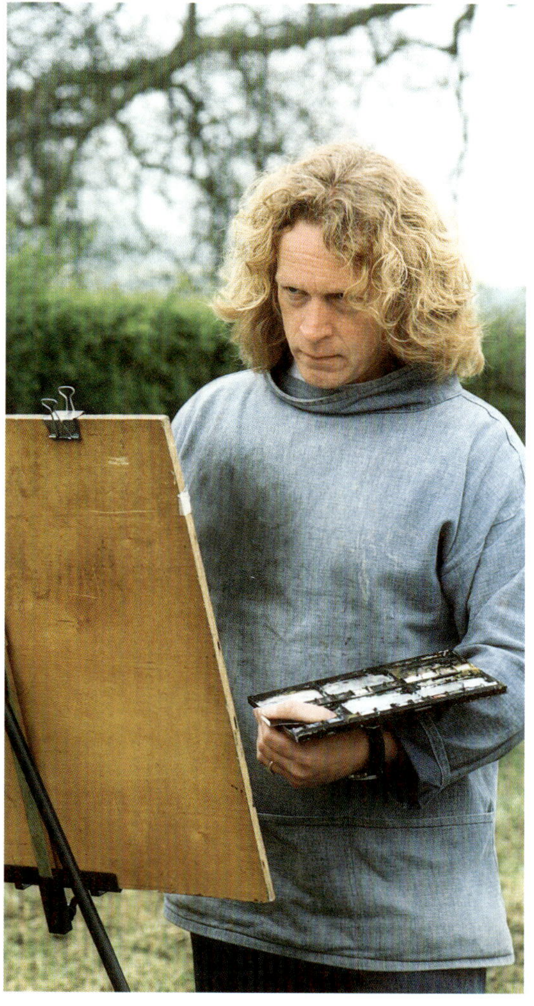

BORN and bred as a country boy in 1953 in the then West Riding of Yorkshire, I had the privilege of a childhood spent playing in the fields and woods, rivers and lakesides around the farm where I was born and brought up. This fuelled an already inbred appreciation of the countryside and the wonders and workings of it. Like most kids I had always drawn and played with coloured pencils but even at a very early age I was always striving to make the drawings better and unlike most kids whose heroes were Batman and Superman and so forth, my heroes were Turner, Flint and Constable. I would wonder at the magic, mood and atmosphere that Turner managed to get into his skies and marvelled how Constable managed to get the effect of his trees.

After a fairly conventional schooling I studied at Lincoln College of Art and finally turned to the medium of water colour. Water colour is the traditional English medium because, as many artists have discovered, it captures the beautiful sense of atmosphere, haziness and dampness and watery skies of the British landscape. In the mid-seventies there was no living to be made out of such art so I turned my attention to catering and had a very long successful career in catering. Whilst still working in that trade I was commissioned by the National Coal Board, as it was then, to paint a series of paintings of pits and pit villages. This led to a very long and fruitful alliance with the Coal Board and they would commission paintings of either dark and gloomy pit scenes or dark overcast moorland scenes. Many of these paintings were presented to prominent MP's of the time who visited various pit situations.

The Coal Board also sponsored my first one-man exhibition which was held at the Hedrow Gallery in Leeds in 1983. It was opened by the Lord Mayor of Leeds and featured on Yorkshire Television. This resulted in all 69 paintings being sold at preview. After that I had successful either one-man or mixed exhibitions up and down the country.

In 1998 I was commissioned by Yorkshire Television to do a brooding type moorland scene for their TV soap "Emmerdale". This I did under the scripted name of 'Nathan Summers'. After this I was asked by Tyne Tees Television to do a short series of painting programmes for their regional series. I made the first three and these proved to be so successful that we made a further nine. As well as being on TV I am now one of the leading demonstrators for Daler-Rowney and demonstrate all over the country and I am also making videos for a company called Teaching Art. Just recently I have made two videos for the Japanese, German, Italian and Netherlands markets which brings us up-to-date. I am now living in both the wilds of Northumberland and Blackheath in London, currently demonstrating painting in both places.

Aims of this book

IN THIS book I will be covering a wide range of subjects from painting outdoors and the problems encountered with this, to painting in the studio. We will be covering the equipment needed for both indoor and outdoors and a range of techniques, and hopefully solving some of the problems that most people encounter with watercolour painting. I am not going to say that watercolour painting is the easiest thing to do; if it were easy then it wouldn't be worthwhile. But with a little practice and some useful hints and tips you will be amazed how quickly your paintings improve. You will be surprised at how quickly you begin to notice things in the landscape that you never noticed before, like for instance the shapes and colours of clouds and skies; the different shapes and colours in trees; and you will soon gather the confidence to put these colours into paintings to create a more lifelike landscape. Grasses are not just green, trees are not just brown and green, and skies are not just blue. All these things you start to realise once you start to paint and look at the world through an artist's eyes.

I spend most of my time painting outdoors. 99% of my paintings are done on location, wherever that may be, and you will be amazed at the difference that the elements can make to the finished landscape painting. A great number of people work from photographs or work indoors in the studio and whilst there is nothing wrong with this, the end result can often be flat and dead. Whereas painting outdoors you get the feel of the life going on around you and this comes over into the painting with a more lively, spontaneous feel to the finished work. You can guarantee that as soon as you set up an easel and start to paint outdoors within a few minutes you'll have one or two people, even a crowd in some cases, watching you paint. This can often be very daunting to the amateur painter so first we need to build up some confidence in our work and that's what this book is intended to do.

I don't intend to baffle the reader with terminology and the drawing skills required will be minimal. So many times in classes and demonstrations I see pupils and students glazing over as soon as the demonstrator starts to talk about disappearing points, perspective and colour mixes. So this kind of thing we shall learn about as we go along and paint. So let's talk about the equipment required for successful painting.

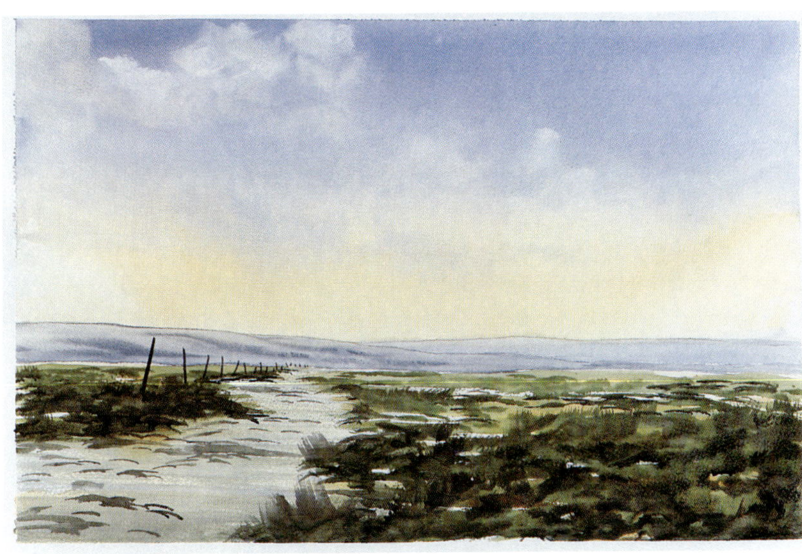

Brushes

THERE are many myths and mysteries surrounding brushes, but basically it's a case of buy what you can afford. It's pointless buying a very expensive wash brush which may cost upwards of £100-£150 unless you are either very wealthy or are going to sell your paintings for a great deal of money. I have heard many painters tell students to buy only the best quality sable brushes, but only very few people can afford to buy the best quality sable brushes. The basic qualities are that a very good sable brush will hold more water and therefore can carry more mixed paint in the brush without having to dip into the water so many times; whereas a synthetic brush holds less water which means that you have to dip in more times. But if you keep your water handy and near enough to the paper then this is no great hardship. Indeed I find that some synthetic brushes are better for doing skies. Because they have a more rigid bristle you can suck out paint to form the clouds easier than with a sable brush. Having said all this, I'm in the fortunate position of being a Daler-Rowney artist and all my materials, including brushes, are supplied and therefore I do use high quality sable brushes and tend to stick mainly with the Diana range which is a beautiful hand-made, high quality, sable brush. But my brushes, even if I had to pay for them, would be worth it because I sell my paintings regularly and also a good quality brush will last for many, many years.

Here are some examples of the brushes that you could use: Firstly these are the brushes that I use regularly – my Diana range. Large wash brush size 14; the medium size brush is a size 10 and the brush below that is a size 8. These are the brushes I tend to use for everything. A brush that I would use occasionally is a rigger brush and here, as you can see, the rigger brush I am using is a synthetic brush and it's size 1. Another brush that I use regularly is again a synthetic brush and this is the Dalon 1½" wash brush, a flat brush which is especially good for large washes such as skies. These five brushes are the brushes that I use all the time and as you can see, two of the five are synthetic. Now, as I mentioned earlier, if you don't want to go to the expense of sable brushes, the four brushes in this picture will give equally pleasing results for a fraction of the price and here shown are again the 1½" Dalon flat brush, a size 5 round brush, a ⅜" flat brush and again the size 1 Dalon rigger brush. Just out on the market is a beautiful mid-priced ranged of brushes by Daler-Rowney and this is the Sapphire range. These brushes will cover all eventualities and they are a mixture of sable and Dalon synthetic. In this picture from left to right is the 1" flat wash brush, the size 14 round brush, the size 8 round brush, a size 2 rigger brush, a size 1 round brush, a size 4 flat brush and a size 2 fan brush. The fan brush we will talk about later when looking at techniques but this range of brushes, as I said, is a beautiful range and will suit most painting techniques in watercolour.

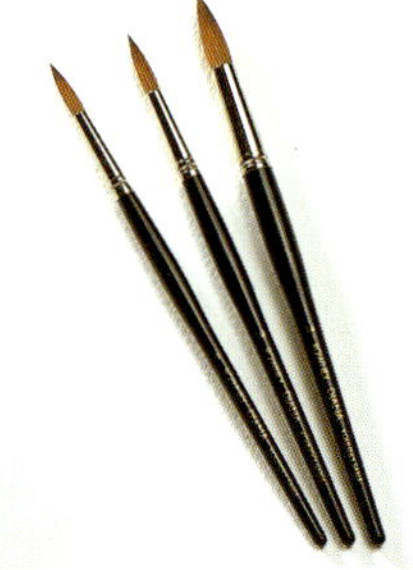

Diana Range

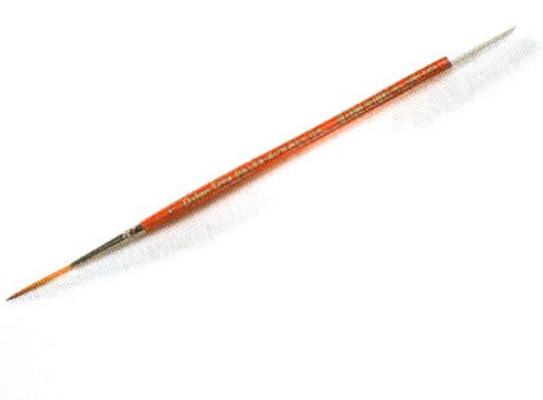

Rigger

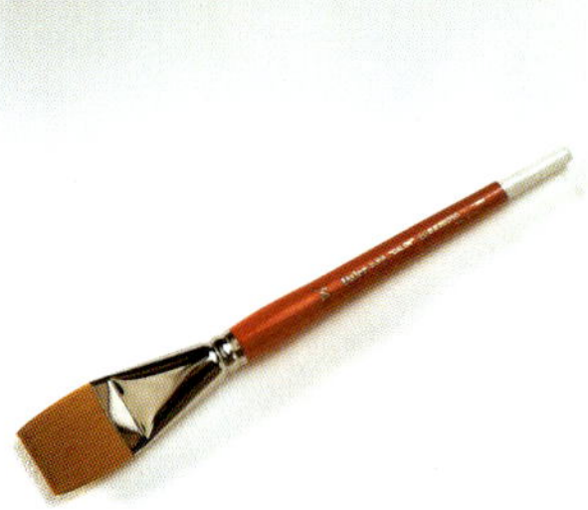

1½" Dalon

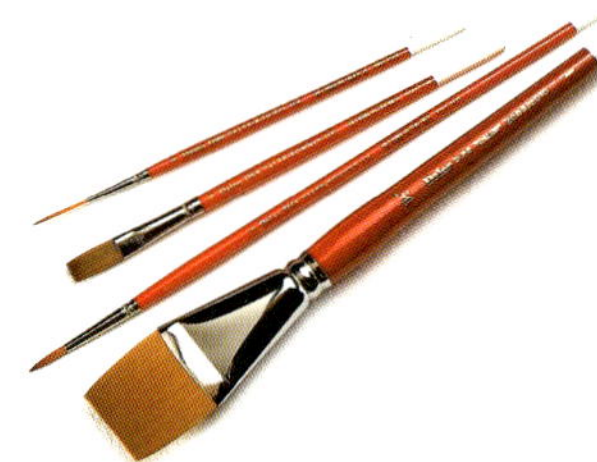

Rigger Size 1 Dalon Flat
Size 5 Round 1½" Flat

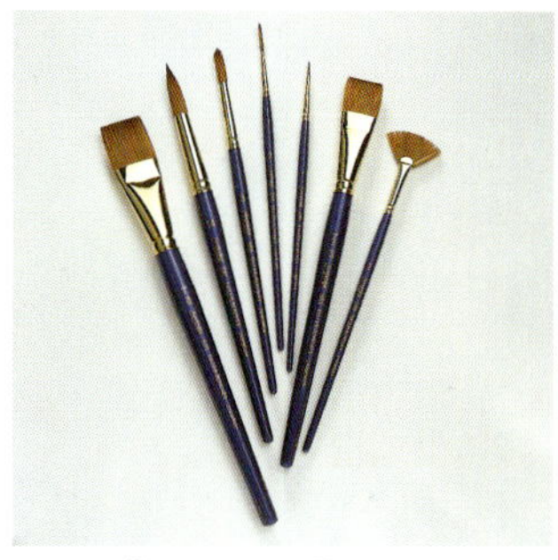

Sapphire Range

Loose Leaf papers
not (left) smooth (right)

Loose Leaf Papers
Saunders Waterford 300lbs

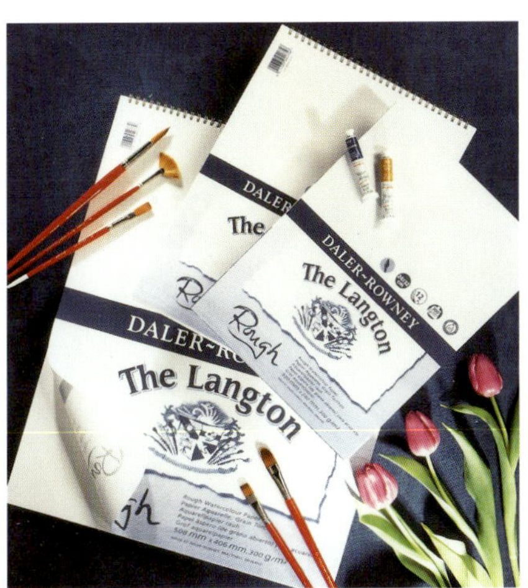

Langton 140lb rough

Papers

THERE is a vast range of paper available to the artist these days and if you go into an art shop you will be overawed at the choice and various qualities of paper, but to simplify matters break it down into three different types of paper.

Firstly there is smooth paper which is obviously smooth and is very good for fine detailed drawings. This is a difficult paper to start and learn to paint watercolouring on.

The next grade of paper is "not". This is a paper with a slight texture to the surface of it and is a good all-round paper which will give you differing effects.

Finally, my favourite paper, which is a rough surface paper or commonly known as just "rough". I tend to use two grades of rough paper; one is the *Saunders Waterford* 300lb rough and the other is the *Langton* 140lb rough. I prefer rough paper because you can get the beautiful effect of light sparkling through as the brush glides across the paper; if you don't press too hard the paint doesn't fall into the indentations and this leaves clear white sparkling through.

All these papers come in a variety of forms. There are the packs which are simply sheets of paper spiral bound. Then also there is loose leaf where you can buy a piece of paper cut down to the size that suits you. Or there are the blocks. Watercolour blocks are probably the most popular because you can paint on these without having to use a board. The pieces of paper are glued together round the edges, leaving just an area where you can stick a knife in to separate them and so you can paint onto the pad and when the painting is finished and completely dry you simply remove that sheet of paper. No need for stretching and no need for boards. I personally prefer to use loose leaf. I buy full imperial sheet size and cut these down to suit myself. Normally my paintings are half imperial sheet size or full imperial sheet size.

The *Langton* 140lb rough watercolour paper is a lovely versatile paper and because it is 140lb weight there is no need to stretch first, just simply tape it to a board and off you go. I find that if I don't put too many washes on, it doesn't buckle or cockle with the amount of water and very importantly, it's also a very inexpensive paper.

The board which I tape my paper to is a simple piece of hardboard 30" square bought from any DIY merchants and most people will cut the board to the size you require. I tape my piece of paper to the board using plain white masking tape. I prefer masking tape because at the end of the painting I like to be able to quickly and easily remove the tape from the paper leaving a white edge so you have an impression of the framed painting. This is somewhat more difficult to do with the brown gum tape as this sticks to the paper's surface.

Speaking of sketch books, there are many different kinds of sketch books on the market, many different grades, qualities and textures.

I prefer to use the hardback book type rather than a pad and mine is an A4 and it contains 150 gramme acid-free cartridge paper. As I have said, there are many types of sketch books on the market; most of them tend to be spiral bound or simply glued to one side. You may find it useful to keep your sketches for posterity – so it is worth investing in a quality book – to look back and remember that day, it really is like an artist's photograph album.

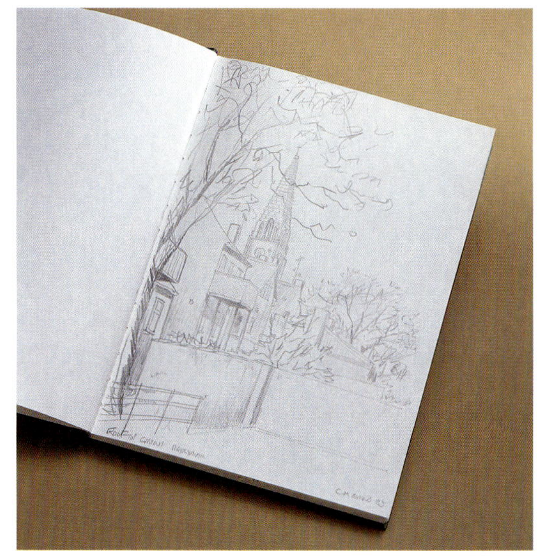

Artist Sketch Book

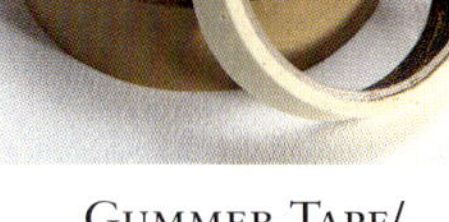

Gummer Tape/
Masking Tape

Easel

THE easel that supports my board and paper is one of the metal tubular type easels which are very easy to erect on site and also very quick and easy to take down if the weather turns nasty. I prefer the metal tubular type because when you tighten the screws to hold the board in position, and at the angle you require, the screws stay in place, unlike the wooden type easels which are more suitable for the studio where once erected they stay.

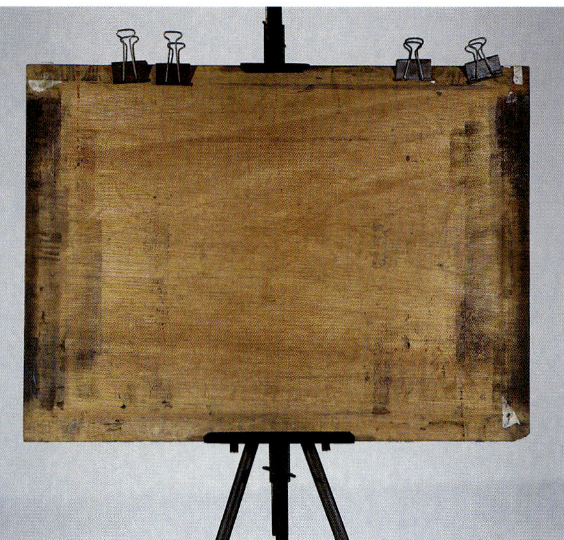

Artist Board

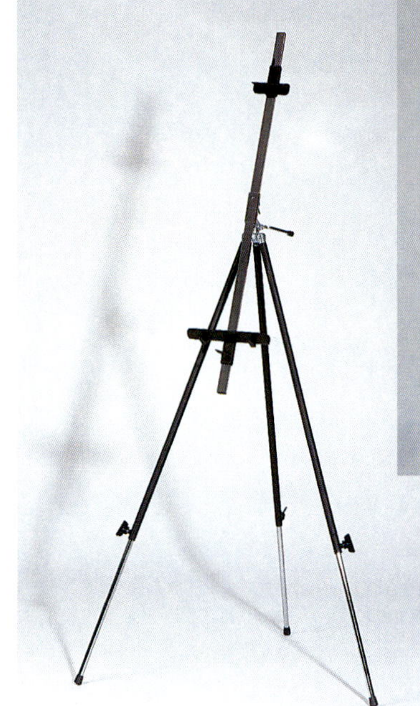

Field Easel

Palette

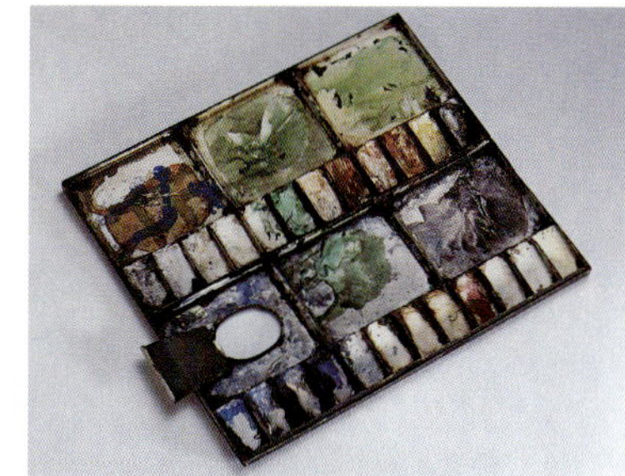

Metal Artist Palette

THE palette I use is a very old fashioned type metal palette and as you will see from this photograph it has various sections to put the paint and then larger areas to mix the paint and a very convenient thumbhold which is covered when the palette is closed. This palette has given me very good service for some 20 years or more and I dread the day when it finally dies. This kind of palette is still available to buy in most art shops, although some of them are slightly larger.

I always use tubed artist quality watercolour paint and so I don't have any need for the type of palette that contains tablets of paint known as "half-pans" or "full pans". So my kind of palette is known as a "mixing palette".

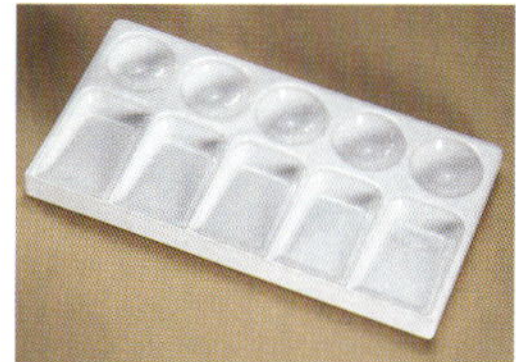

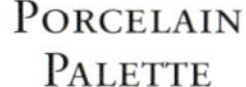

Porcelain Palette

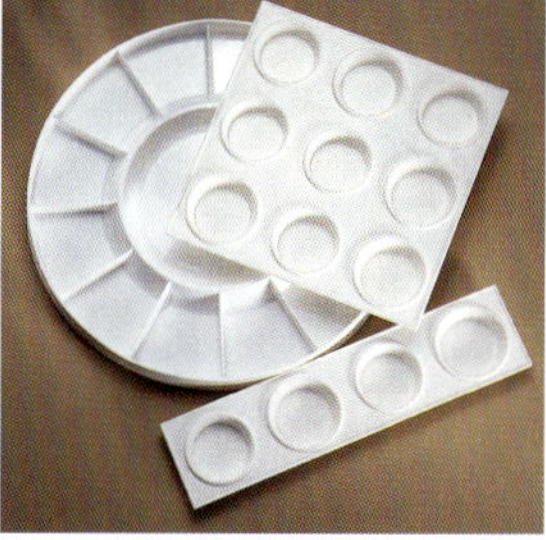

Plastic Palettes

Palettes come in all kinds of shapes, sizes and qualities. I would always prefer to use the metal palettes although there are some very high quality plastic palettes to be had in art shops. I have nothing against plastic palettes but one tip that I would say is very important and that is not to buy the cheapest plastic palettes. Some of these can be as little as 50p or 75p but spend that little extra two or three pounds, or even five pounds because, as you may know, plastic is a by-product from the petroleum industry and the cheaper and thinner they are the chemicals are nearer to the surface of the plastic. Therefore these tend to react with the watercolour paint and you may get splitting in the palette whilst you are trying to mix the paint, resulting in that rainbow effect that you often see on the tarmac when diesel's been spilt and then water is added to it.

Another kind of mixing palette is the china or porcelain type. These are very nice for in the studio but not very practical when it comes to painting outdoors when things can be easily dropped and once dropped these are broken for ever and tend to be very expensive.

The other types of palette are the kinds I referred to earlier as the ones that carry the half or full pans of paint. I don't have much experience of this type of palette because I, as I said earlier, always use tubed paints but these are a very popular type of palette and are especially good when contained within the little field packs or hand-held painting kits which come complete with pad, pencil, brush and paints and usually a little water container, all nicely packaged together. The reason why I prefer to use tubed paints as opposed to tablets or pans of paint is because with a pan, either full or half, you have to dip into the paint and the water so many times when doing a very large wash, as opposed to tubes whereby you squeeze the desired amount into the mixing area, water it down and then just dip into it with your big brush and use big, bold strokes onto the paper. This is impossible with pans as you need to keep getting enough paint onto the brush from the pan.

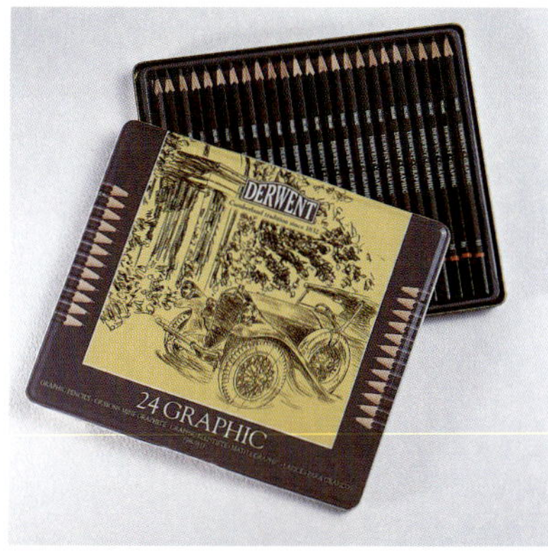

Pencils

ONTO pencils and this is probably the shortest part of the book because I really don't do that much drawing and the drawing that I do tends to be mainly outline drawing. There is no shading required therefore different grades of pencils are useless to me. I tend to use a 2B pencil, or an HB pencil for my outlines and then it's on with the paint.

The only time that I would tend to spend any more time than this drawing is if I were actually drawing in my sketch book in times of inclement weather or when I simply haven't got time to do my paintings outdoors.

For this type of drawing I have one tin of pencils which is a tin of Derwent pencils and it contains 12 graphic sketching pencils. These are a 9B, 8B, 7B, 6B, 5B, 4B, 3B, 2B, a B an HB an F and an H.

Paints

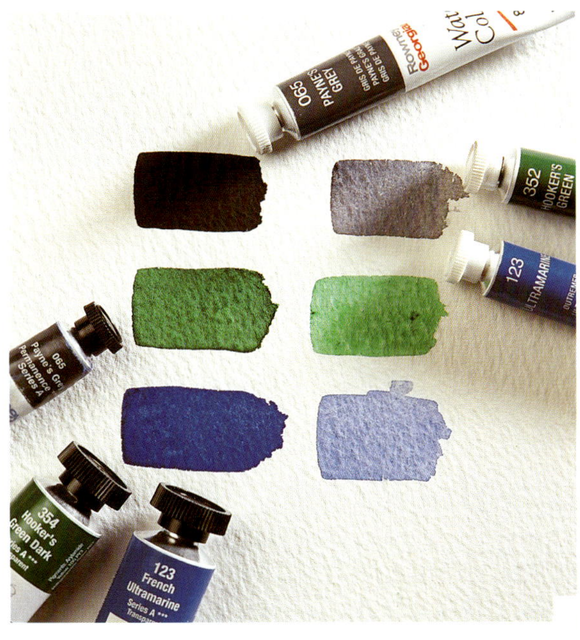

Here are some examples of all those colours laid out for you and how they look on paper:

I TALKED earlier about my preference for using tubed paints rather than pans. Amongst the tubed paints there are also two grades, student's quality and artist's quality, the main difference being that in 20 years time from now when someone has paid a great deal of money for one of my paintings the painting will still be there. If I were to use student's quality paint, the painting would fade a lot quicker. Having said that, in only a few colours is there a slight difference in the depth of colour between student's quality paint and artist's quality paint. These are namely French Ultramarine Blue, Paynes Grey and Hookers Green, and here are some examples of those three colours.

This is because in the artist's quality paint it is pure pigment and therefore the colour is brighter, stronger, more vibrant. In student's quality paint you often see underneath the main colour in brackets it will say "hue", this means artificial colour.

When you first start painting don't confuse yourself with too many colours. This is a common mistake where people buy every colour that they can get their hands on. Don't be drawn into this one, keep to a fairly limited palette. That way you won't be tempted to experiment with too many colours at an early stage and the result is often too many colours, too much mud. My list of main colours are as follows:

- ❑ French Ultramarine Blue
- ❑ Coeruleum Blue
- ❑ Yellow Ochre
- ❑ Burnt Sienna
- ❑ Raw Sienna
- ❑ Raw Umber
- ❑ Warm Sepia
- ❑ Hookers Green Dark
- ❑ Cadmium Yellow
- ❑ Alizarin Crimson
- ❑ Light Red

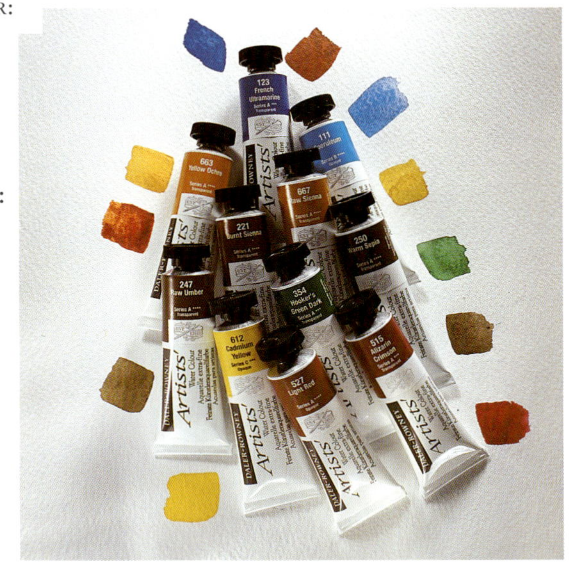

With these basics you can mix a massive array of different vibrant colours and with these colours I paint most of my landscapes from Mediterranean bright blue skies to stormy Northumberland moorland scenes.

You will notice that not in this list are black and white. White is a colour that really shouldn't be in the artist's paint box and if it is it should be just for mixing down with. If you need white in your painting then there is no purer white than the white of the paper, so leave the areas that you want to show white without paint. This you can do by simply avoiding the area or you can use masking fluid. Black is a colour that kills an area stone dead. Wherever you put black in a painting area that area is dead, no light can get in. You can mix a much better black using either Hookers Green Dark and Alizarin Crimson or French Ultramarine Blue and Burnt Sienna. These are very broad blacks, they are not dead.

Brush Techniques

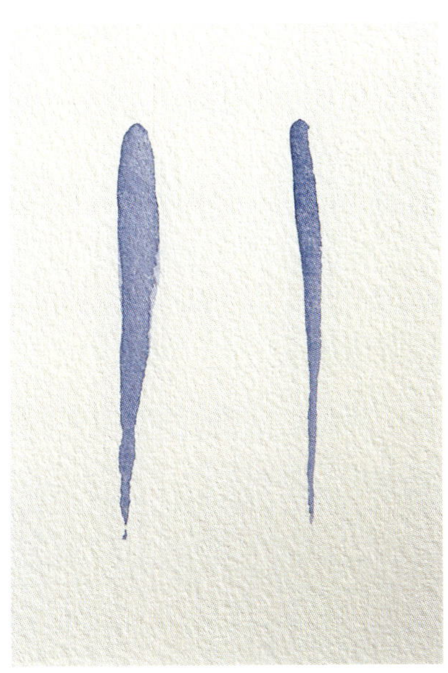

Round Brush

TO GIVE you some idea of what the different brushes can do here are a few examples of various techniques.

A round brush will give you a good broad stroke but as you lift the brush upwards away from the paper this broad stroke gets thinner until eventually it becomes a fine line, all with one stroke of the brush. Obviously the varying degree of broad stroke to fine line differs with the size of round brush used.

A large flat brush is mainly used for large washes but also can be used for grasses, in the way shown here. Again these strokes or grasses, by using the side of the brush, can be larger or smaller depending on the size of brush that you use. People tend to think that a specific brush is for a specific purpose but with a little practice and experimenting with your own brushes you will get to see what each individual brush can do.

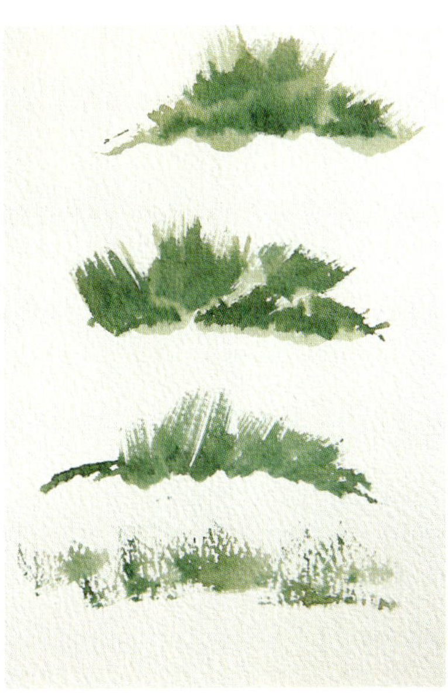

Flat Wash Brush

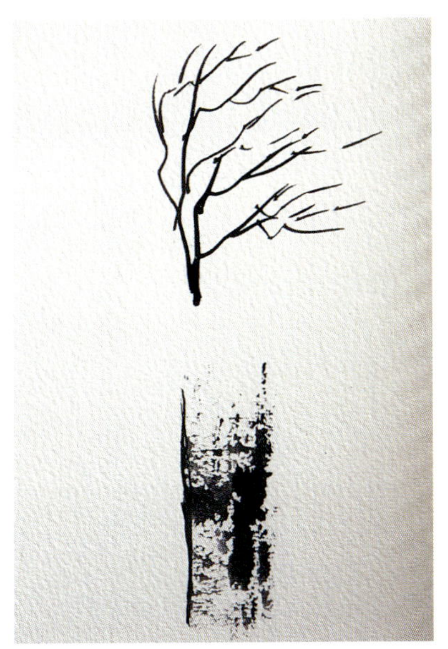

Rigger Brush

Here is a rigger brush, commonly used for twigs and very fine detail. It gets its name from the obvious, rigger, and it was designed to paint rigging on sailing ships. As well as painting twigs and fine detail, as pictured here, you could also again use the side of this brush which gives a lovely effect of mosses and growth on the side of a tree.

A very specific brush is a fan brush and is ideal for grasses and trees, as in this picture.

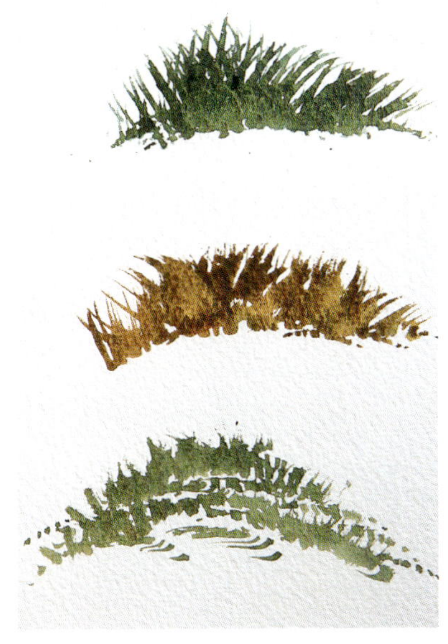

Fan Brush

Painting – *Moorland Scene*

NOW, let's get down to some painting. I intend to build you up very steadily using large washes first of all. As we progress through the book we'll get slightly more complicated using different techniques and brush strokes.

This first scene is a straightforward moorland scene, large sky, small foreground and this is a scene that is typical of the Northumberland moorlands that I spend a great deal of my time painting.

As you can see from the photograph, the drawing is a very simple drawing; just outline the main parts of the picture and the path which leads us from the foreground into the middle distance of the painting. This is all the drawing that you need for a broad landscape. There is no need to make it any more complicated.

Now I am going to start my main skywash by wetting the whole of the paper from the top into the distant hills and for this I need plenty of water, really flood the paper. At this stage I will mop up surplus water from the bottom of my wet area, first to avoid drips and it is quite important at this stage to remember to keep your board at about a 45° angle because as the paint runs down the paper this is going to help you to form the sky.

The first colour I am going in with is a fairly weak wash of Yellow Ochre. I have wet the Yellow Ochre in my palette so that it's really quite watery and put quite a lot of that all the way across from left to right, the bottom third of the sky. On top of this I am putting about the same strength mixture of Burnt Sienna and I am putting that above the Yellow Ochre so that it runs down into the Yellow Ochre.

In the next photograph you can see that I have now added a mixture of French Ultramarine Blue with a tiny touch of Burnt Sienna. Not too much Burnt Sienna otherwise it will turn it a dark grey colour and all I want to do is "knock off" the bright blueness of the French Ultramarine Blue.

Now as you can see, the blue is running into the Burnt Sienna and the Burnt Sienna is running into the yellow giving this wonderful hazy feeling of clouds falling down from the sky.

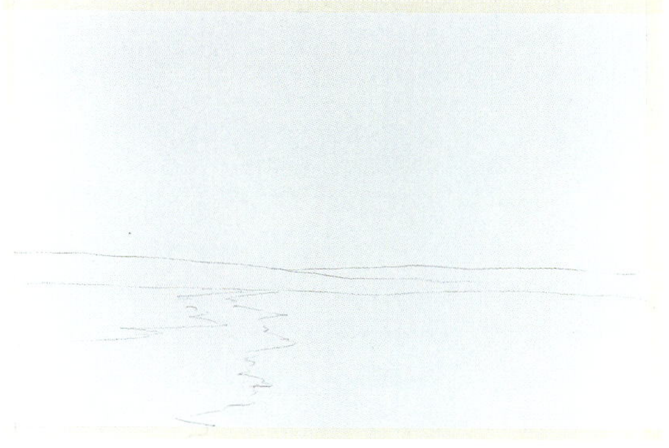

OUTLINE DRAWING

YELLOW OCHRE WASH AND BURNT SIENNA

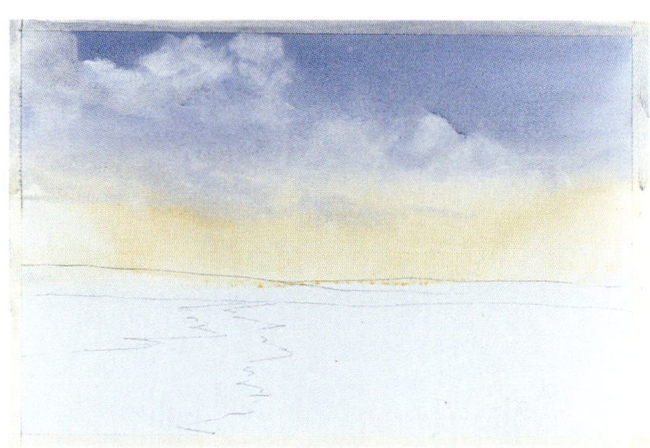

FRENCH ULTRAMARINE BLUE WITH TOUCH OF BURNT SIENNA

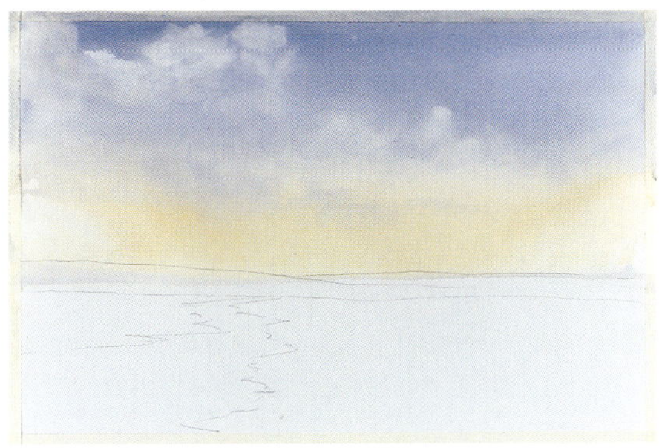

Sucking Out the Water

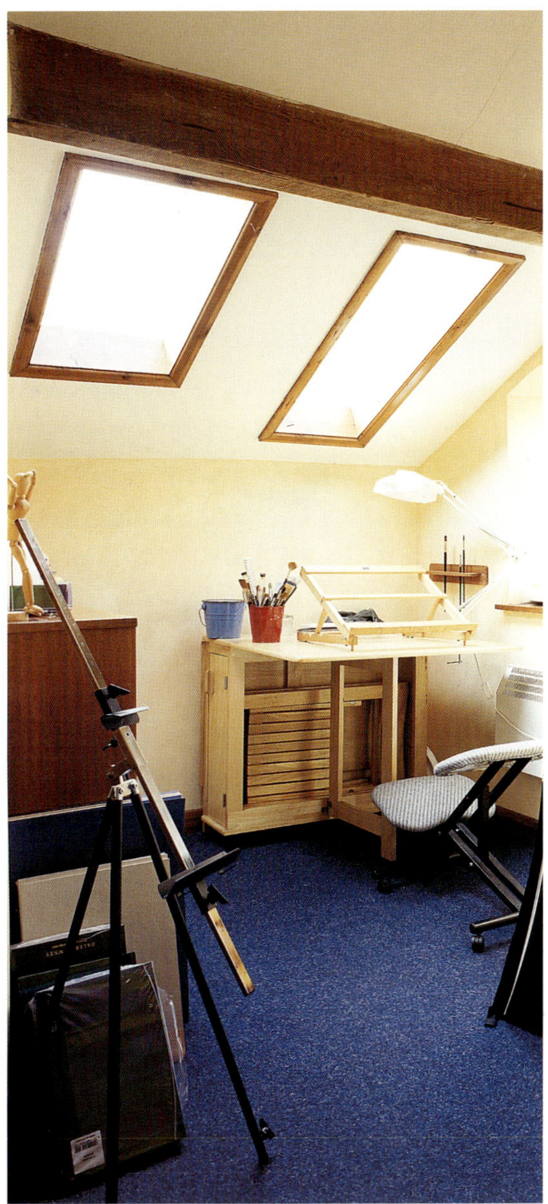

Artist's Studio

AT THIS next stage I have cleaned out my large brush and still using the large flat washbrush and squeezing out surplus water, all I need to do is just run across the sky and suck out some of the paint that's already on the paper. It's quite important to do this whilst it's still very damp otherwise you will get hard edges around your clouds and as you can see from this photograph, the clouds are really quite fluffy and light. This I have achieved by just sucking out the water with a fairly stiff Dalon brush; and that's your first skywash finished.

There, that wasn't too complicated was it?

Whilst my sky is drying I will tell you about the indoor easel that I am using. This is a straightforward table easel and it's a bit like the old fashioned deckchairs – you just lift it up and slot the piece of wood into one of the grooves to give you the desired angle for your painting. Quite often, even indoors, I paint standing up at my easel but not a lot of people like to stand up at an easel all the time. This kind of table easel is ideal for just fitting onto any worksurface, just sit down and paint. Another tip for painting indoors is to either sit by a window where there is an ample supply of natural daylight or to buy one of the many daylight bulbs that are on offer. In my studio I have one of the large magnifying glasses with a daylight bulb fixed to the inside of it and this is on an angle poised type lamp and I have this clamped to the table above my table easel. The set up you can see from the photograph of the inside of my studio is very comfortable and is one which has worked for me for many years.

NOW BACK to the painting. As you can see from this next photograph once the sky has dried I paint in the distant hills and the distant hills are more or less the same colour as the sky, which remember is French Ultramarine Blue with a tiny touch of Burnt Sienna. The furthest hill has got a lot more water into the mixture to make it a lot weaker. This gives the impression that the weaker hill is much further away, therefore creating more distance into the painting.

At this stage it is important to say that I tend to use, most of the time, what's known as the key colour system. That's just like cooking – you put a pinch of salt into most things when you're cooking and so with the colour system the main colour of the sky, which in this case is French Ultramarine Blue and Burnt Sienna for the blue areas, is repeated throughout most of the painting. A little touch of that blue and Burnt Sienna mixture is put into most colours so that everything is blending in together and sitting well together to create the whole picture. Because if you're not careful you could end up with a sky from the South of France, a long distance from Scotland and middle distance from Yorkshire and a foreground from Cornwall, all in the same picture and it doesn't look right together. Things are opposing each other but the key colour system, as I said makes everything blend in together and sit well.

Once I've painted the colour onto the hills then with a washed out and dried brush I then suck a little bit of paint out of the hills in flowing diagonal movement, in much the same way as we sucked the colour out of the sky to create the clouds. This forms some movement to the hills; it sculpts them.

Once my hills have dried it's time to move forward and as you can see from the next photograph I've roughly dropped in some Yellow Ochre, again remember this colour was in the sky and I fill in the majority of the path with Yellow Ochre but leaving some of the white sparkling paper showing through. This is the advantage of using rough textured paper, you can leave the white sparkly bits showing. I've also put the Yellow Ochre into some of the grasses and foreground areas.

In this next photograph you can see that I've done much the same thing with Burnt Sienna. Just filling in some of those white areas with loose, watery strokes of Burnt Sienna; well watered down. But I haven't put this Burnt Sienna into the path, I'm leaving the path to dry now until the final strokes.

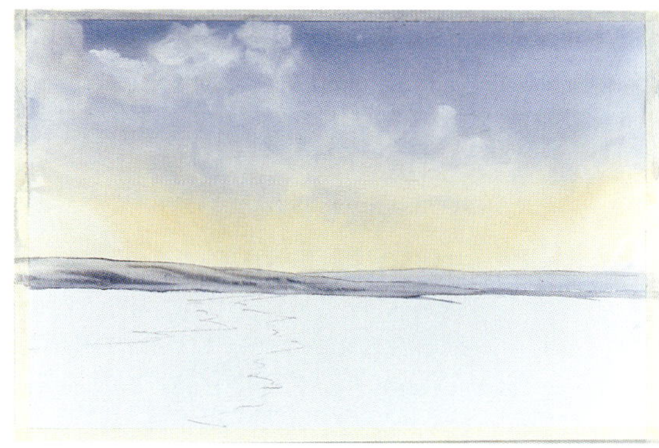

Distant Hills

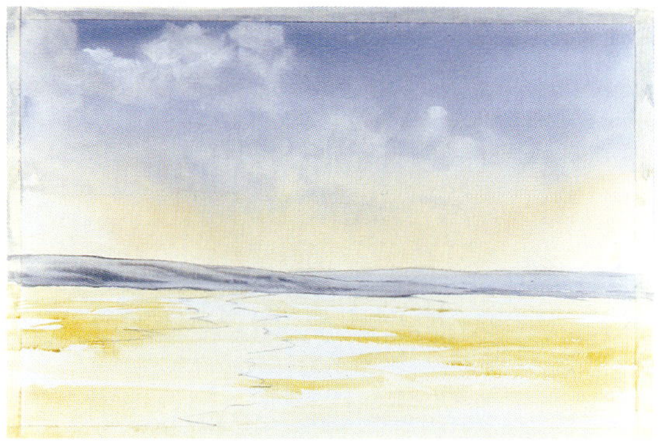

Yellow Ochre into grass

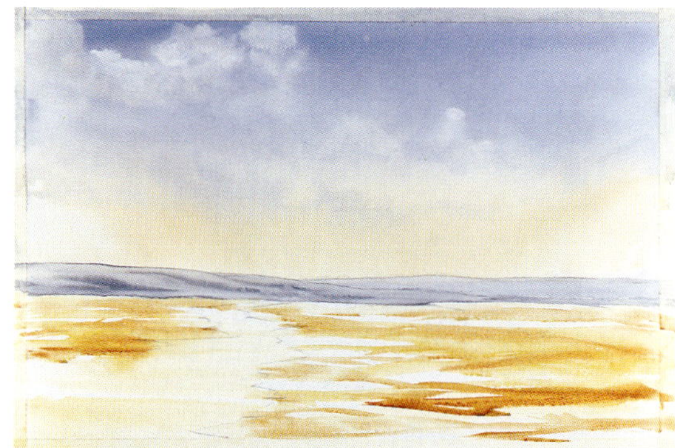

Watery Strokes of Burnt Sienna

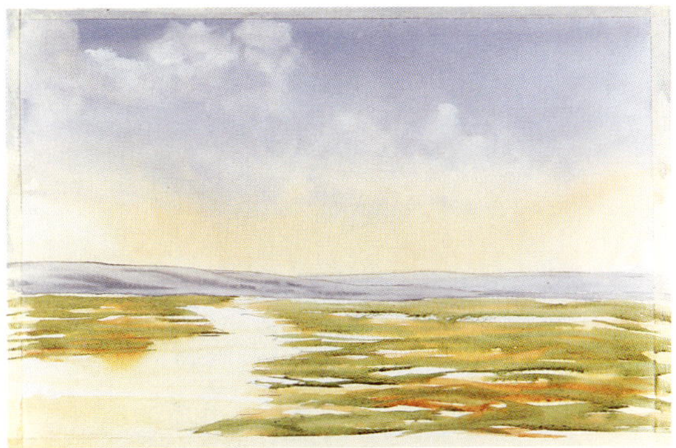

Hooker Green Dark with Burnt Sienna

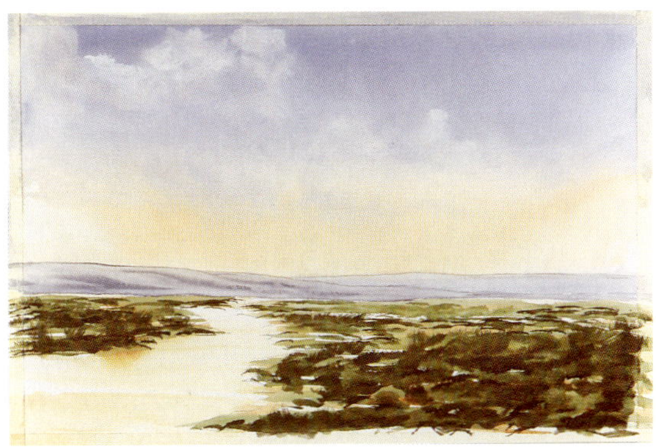

Adding French Ultramarine Blue

AS YOU can see in this next photograph, it's the first time I am using green and I'm starting to fill in some of the moorland grasses. This green is achieved by mixing Hookers Green Dark with a touch of Burnt Sienna. It's always handy to keep a spare piece of paper at the side of your easel to test the mixed colours before you actually apply them to the painting. That way you're not going to get mistakes in colour mixing.

Again, I'm leaving the path alone with this colour and just applying the green to either side of the path. It's interesting to note that at this stage I am actually painting from the foreground away into the background. That way I can dip my brush into the ready mixed colour and as I stroke along going further back into the distance the colour gets weaker as it runs out of my brush and I'm helping myself to create a more distant look – the green is weaker in the distance. All of these colours are added whilst the first colour in the grasses is still damp so the Yellow Ochre is wet, the Burnt Sienna is put on top of the wet Yellow Ochre and then the green is put in whilst the other two colours are still slightly damp.

Once my grasses have dried slightly I am going to go in with some actual tufts of grass. To achieve the darker green I'm using more or less the same mixture which, if you remember was Hookers Green Dark with Burnt Sienna but now I'm putting a touch of French Ultramarine Blue in. Remember that sky colour is going into the grass. This will help to darken the green and make it richer.

At this stage many people make the mistake of going to a very small brush and actually painting blades of grass.

Instead of doing this, and making the picture too busy and fussy, I'm going to use my big wash brush and stroke upwards so my brush touches the paper. I flick it up and this creates the effect of tufts of grass rather than individual blades of grass.

Now that's the majority of my grasses finished and so it's back to the path.

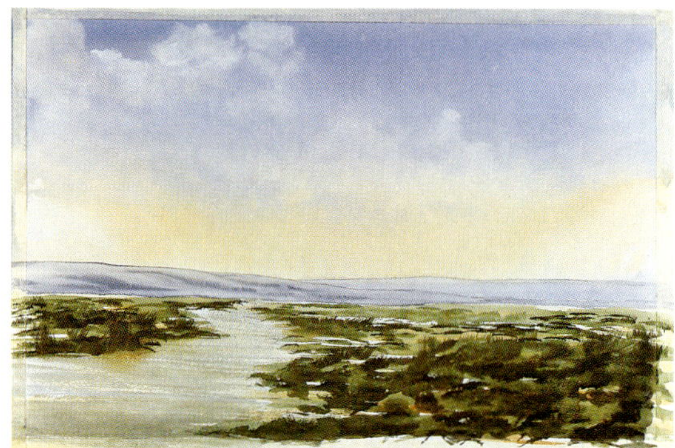

Creating Damp Looking Path

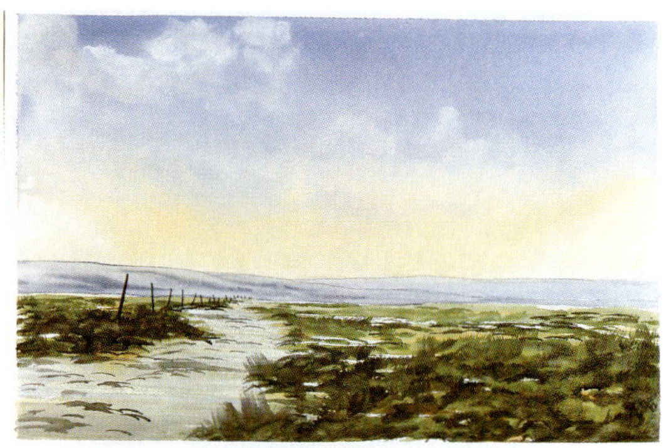

Adding the Vertical Posts

ONCE MY grasses have dried, as you can see from this next picture, I actually stroke over the Yellow Ochre which I previously put onto the path, with a mixture of French Ultramarine Blue and Burnt Sienna; remember that's the sky colour again. I've loosely stroked over the Yellow Ochre so that now I'm leaving sparkles of Yellow Ochre showing through my blue mixture and also sparkles of the original white paper showing through the whole thing. This gives the effect of a nice damp looking path.

Here's a little tip about some perspective. To get some distance into a painting it's always useful, even if they're not there, to invent some verticals of some kind into the painting. As you can see from this next picture I've actually put some posts at the side of the path, kind of growing up from the tufts of grass and each post is slightly smaller than the first as they fade off into the distance. This takes you into the painting and gives you some impression of distance.

The mixtures of paint I use for these posts is again the sky colour; French Ultramarine Blue and Burnt Sienna but this time very heavy on both colours and then add the water and it's almost a black colour. But as I've said previously, unlike black this mixture isn't dead. Once I finish the posts, in the same colour I put a few brush strokes into the path, giving the impression of a few rough bits or stones in the path. Also a few touches of this colour where the grass meets the path gives the impression of shadow and shade in the rough tufts of grass. There, that's our first painting finished. Now that wasn't too difficult was it comprising mainly washes and big broad brush strokes?

The Importance of Skies

I CONSIDER the sky to be the most important element in any painting. The sky is the part of the painting that sets the mood, atmosphere and the style of the painting. It is, if you like, the eyes of the painting. Look into someone's eyes and you know how they feel and the same can be said about a painting; look at the sky and you know exactly what the atmosphere and mood of the day was. You can put practically any colour in a sky and get away with it, it will look right as long as it is mixed in the right way with the right elements. How often have you heard people say "I saw a sunset the other night and if I'd painted that in those colours you would have looked at it and said 'that can't be real'". But it is real and the sky contains so many different colours, all you have to do is look and observe; but look with an artist's eye and you'll see colours in the sky that you never dreamed possible.

Here are a few examples of quick, broad washed skies containing many different colours but setting different moods and different atmospheres for different paintings.

When painting on location I tend to look at the general overall colour and feel to the sky rather than try to capture individual clouds. Remember clouds are moving all the time and the sky is changing all the time so don't try to capture all these, just look at the feel and the colour of the sky – is it light? Is it dark? Is it thundery? Try to capture this rather than individual clouds.

In this first picture you will see a fairly overcast sky which is typical of the skies that I am painting all the time above the Northumberland Moors. In this sky the main colours for the top areas are French Ultramarine Blue and Burnt Sienna, a touch of Burnt Sienna on its own and a little bit of French Ultramarine Blue, well washed down at the bottom part of the sky. This gives a general overcast feeling.

In the next picture is a particularly thundery sky and for this sky in top areas I have used a very strong mixture of French Ultramarine Blue with Burnt Sienna, mixed in with a little bit of Warm Sepia, whilst the overall sky is still very, very wet. In the bottom areas a tiny touch of Yellow Ochre just to add a little bit of light in the bottom and then whilst the sky is still very damp, using a clean wash brush, squeeze the surplus water out of it and take out some of those turbulent looking clouds.

OVERCAST SKY

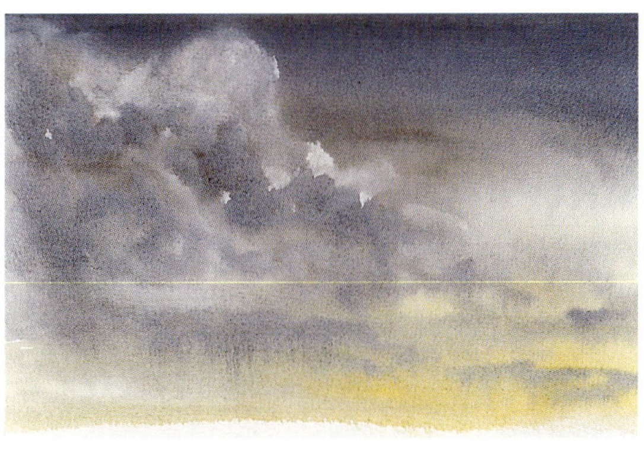

THUNDERY SKY

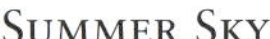

Summer Sky

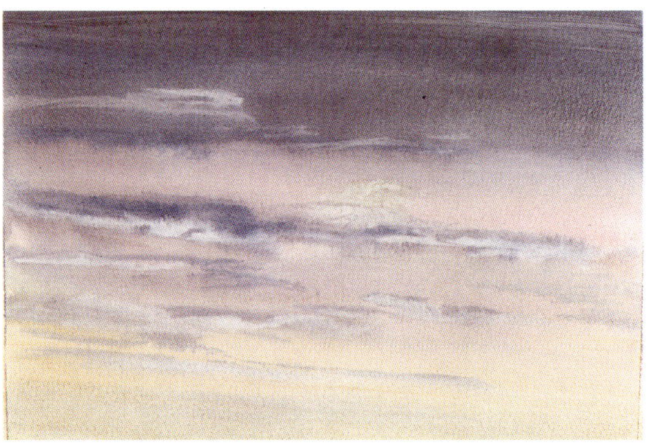

Sunset Sky

IN THE third picture, this sky is a particularly summery one with big, billowy clouds. The top area is Coeruleum Blue, with a tiny touch of Alizarin Crimson mixed into it and let it run down, keeping that board at a 45° angle so the water is running down. I then add a little bit of Yellow Ochre to the bottom to create my light and then with a very large wash brush squeeze out surplus water and take out those big billowy clouds. Then to the bottom of the clouds I add a very weak mixture of French Ultramarine Blue with Light Red. This is a very warm type of a grey colour. Plenty of water into this and just drop it into the bottom of the clouds, which kind of signifies the bottom of the clouds. This is the shadow cast by one cloud onto another cloud. This I hope gives the feeling of a typical summery sky and you can imagine the type of landscape that you would paint under this; nice and watery with summery trees and a blue distance.

In the next picture you will see a sunset sky, and although this may look difficult, remember for all of these skies I have just used one very large wash brush and big bold strokes. Whilst the paper is still very wet I drop in Yellow Ochre in the bottom areas and then a touch of Burnt Sienna above the Yellow Ochre and then above the Burnt Sienna some fairly well watered down Alizarin Crimson.

Let all these colours merge together, remember keeping your board at a 45° angle to let the colours run into each other. Whilst all this is still very wet I get a very strong mixture of French Ultramarine Blue with Burnt Sienna and drop this in on the top line of the painting. Now let this colour start to run down into the other colours. One thing to remember about sunset skies – rather than have big fluffy clouds, they have fairly straight horizontal clouds. So, with the edge of my large wash brush I grab some of this colour from the top and come across horizontally, fairly straight strokes, but don't have them all unbroken, break some of them so they get much weaker as they get towards the bottom of the sky until they fade away to practically nothing. One thing to remember about sunset skies is going back to what I said earlier – you should be observing things all the time. If you look at a fairly big expanse of sunset sky you will see that the clouds are lit from the bottom rather than from the top. So don't take out big fluffy clouds at the top of these dark lines that we have done, just take out a thin sliver of paint from the underside of these dark clouds. This will make it look like the sun has already gone and is lighting up the clouds from underneath rather than on top. That will give you the true feel of a sunset sky.

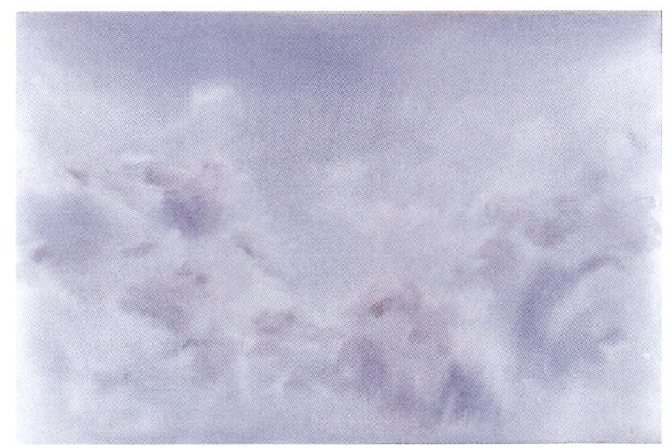

TO EMPHASISE the importance of the sky in painting this next little picture is practically all sky, with just the addition of a little top of the mountain peeping out of the clouds. Now here we have a perfectly acceptable finished painting which is practically nothing but sky. For this painting again I have my board at a 45° angle and I totally saturate the paper with water, then working downwards I add my mixture of French Ultramarine Blue with the tiniest little touch of Burnt Sienna, keeping it still a bright blue colour. Let this start to run down and then towards the bottom areas add little touches here and there of French Ultramarine Blue mixed with Light Red to add a little greyness to the bottom areas of the cloud. I then, with my large wash brush, take out the sky colour to form the clouds as we have done in previous skies. Now with a mixture of French Ultramarine Blue and Light Red and plenty of water I just paint the outline of the mountain top, weakening here and there with the addition of more water and taking out colour with my large wash brush to give the impression of snow capped hills. Then in the bottom areas of my mountain I strengthen the colour of French Ultramarine Blue and Light Red to form types of shadows in the snow and craggy hillside. Now with the addition of French Ultramarine Blue and Burnt Sienna to form a very strong dark colour, these strokes are going to be hard shadows forming cracks and crevices in the mountainside. Now that's the painting finished. A very simple painting consisting of mainly sky with just the addition of a few darker colours.

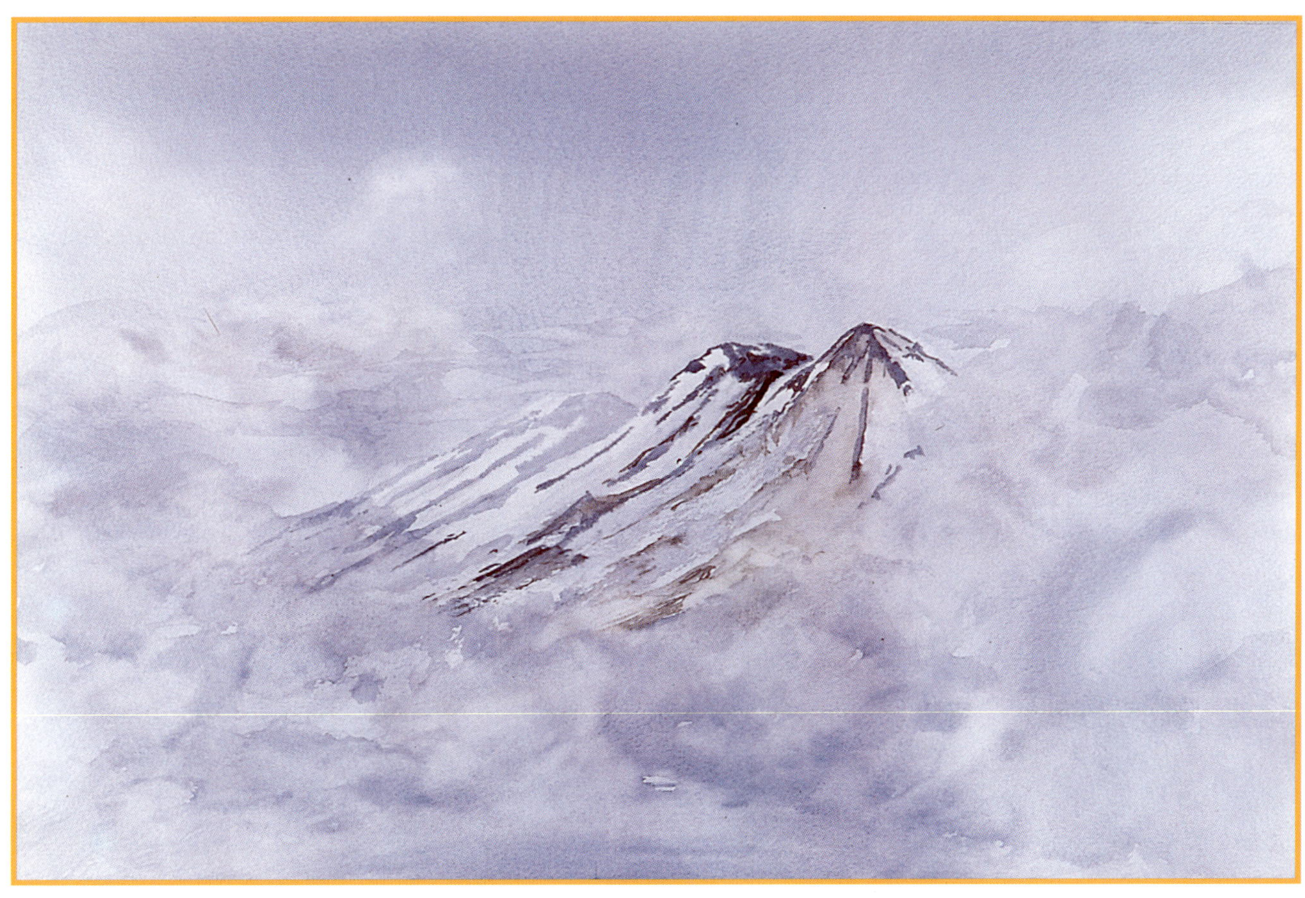

Trees – *Fir Trees and Scots Pines*

BEFORE we go on to the next painting I'd like to give you a few hints and tips on trees, and we'll start with fir trees and Scots Pines. Trees are a subject which mystify and terrify many people trying to paint. But we can break these down and simplify them in a few simple steps. For these I'm using a small flat edged wash brush and I am starting with a simple pole and this colour is a mixture of Burnt Sienna and French Ultramarine Blue to form a very dark grey colour. Now as you will see the pole is thicker at the bottom and thinner at the top. Using the corner of my small flat brush I am just putting a few tiny strokes at the top, getting broader as they come down so that towards the bottom they become long, horizontal strokes. For these horizontal strokes I am using a mixture of Hookers Green Dark with a tiny touch of Burnt Sienna just to darken the green a little bit. Underneath these horizontal strokes I'm going in with a mixture of my dark colour, the same colour used for the pole, French Ultramarine Blue with a touch of Burnt Sienna, and this is forming a shadow underneath the main blocks of leaves. I put it into context by putting a small stroke of green at the base of the pole and it looks as if it's a fir tree growing out of the ground.

To build a single fir tree up into a small forest of fir trees is just as simple. I'm starting off with exactly the same strokes as I did for an individual fir tree but using French Ultramarine Blue on its own and I'm doing lots of poles. Whilst this colour is still slightly damp I'm darkening the colour a little bit by putting a tiny touch of Burnt Sienna into my French Ultramarine Blue and doing some more poles on top of the first lot. This is giving the impression that there are darker trees in front of the more distant lighter trees. Now I am starting with my horizontal strokes again, using French Ultramarine Blue and Burnt Sienna, a few tiny touches at the top growing bigger as they come towards the bottom of the tree. Notice at this stage that I am letting quite a few of the light blue poles show through at the tops of the darker poles. This way it looks as if you are looking through foreground trees to the distant trees.

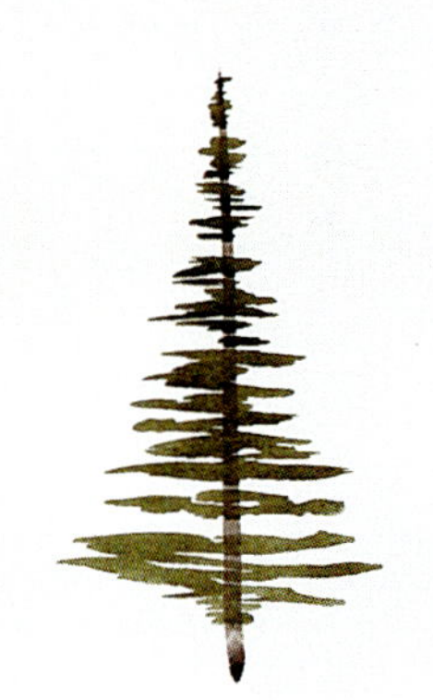

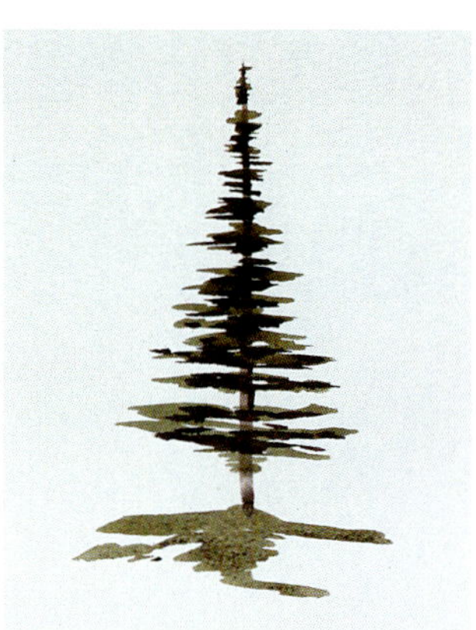

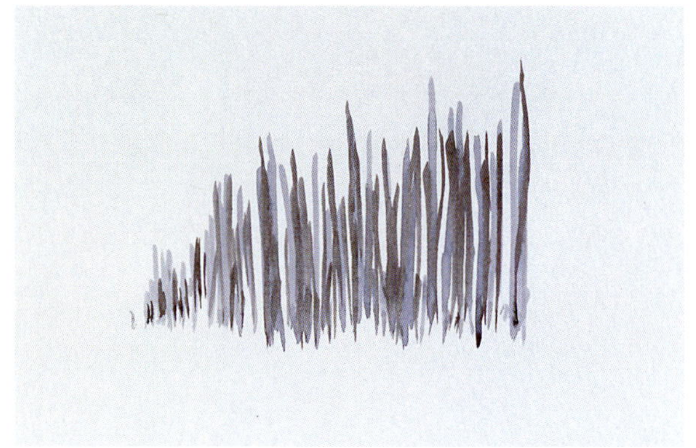

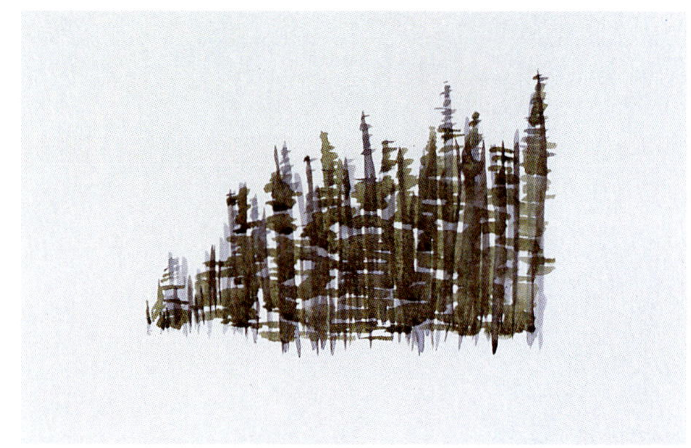

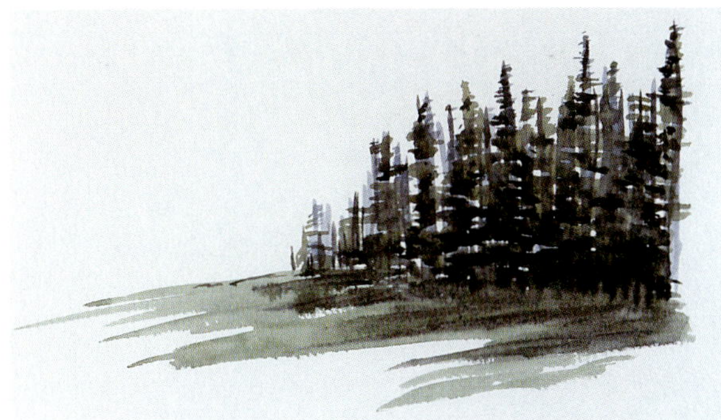

NOW I'M mixing my Hookers Green Dark and Burnt Sienna and putting a few strokes horizontally from the base of the trees working upwards so that towards the top they're just tiny dots of colour here and there. I'm going in with my shadow colour now, which is French Ultramarine Blue with a touch of Burnt Sienna, to darken it a little bit and I'm putting shadows underneath the main leaf blocks just as I did on the individual fir tree. I'm also touching in at the base of the poles in the foreground with this very dark colour – this creates a bit of shadow as the main leaf block casts shadow on the trunks of the trees and now, again to put it into context, put a quick stroke of green at the base of the main block of trees and it looks like you've got a pine forest growing out of the grass.

For Scots Pine it's even less complicated. Notice with the same colour mixture, French Ultramarine Blue and Burnt Sienna, I'm again drawing my pole, slightly thicker at the base than at the top, but at the top now I'm just putting a few twigs coming out from the top of the tree almost horizontally and getting slightly bigger as they go towards the base of the tree. But you'll notice that these twigs stop about a third of the way down the tree with just the odd scratchy little bit of twig towards the base. I'm again using my small flat edged brush and now I'm mixing my colours of Hookers Green Dark and Burnt Sienna and with a few simple strokes just touching in on top of the twigs that I've already painted to create a bit of leaf block towards the top of the tree, getting much finer as it comes down to the base, about a third of the way down the pole. With my shadow colour again of French Ultramarine Blue and Burnt Sienna I'm putting a few touches of shadow underneath the main leaf block and that's my pine tree finished.

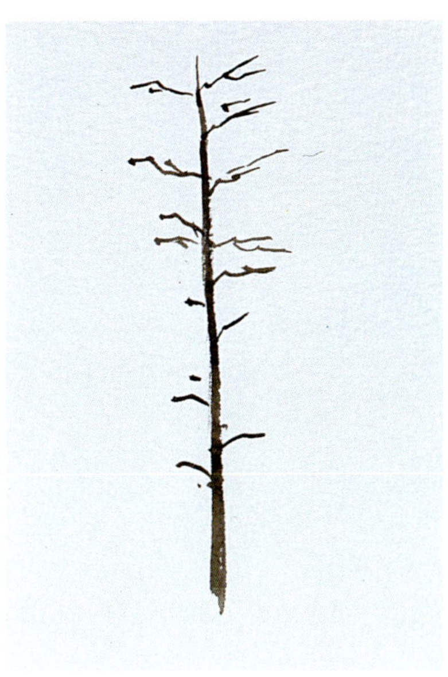

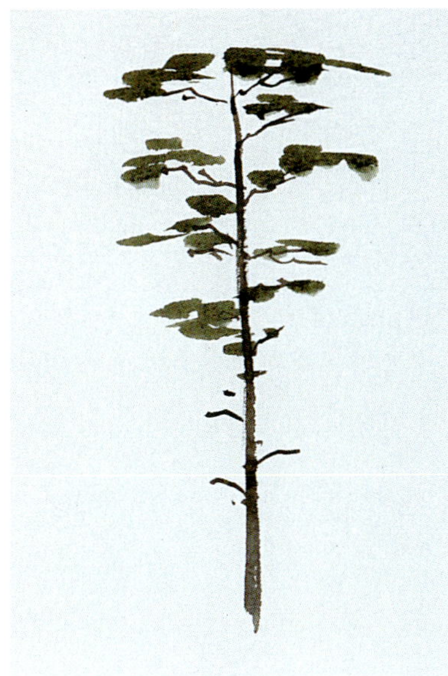

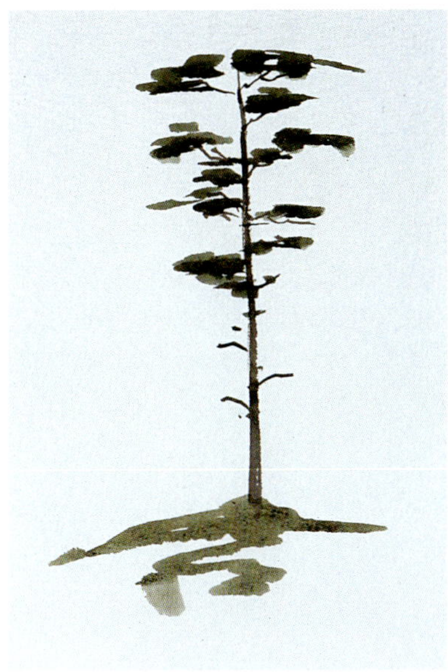

Painting – *Forest & Lake*

AND SO it's on to the next painting. You will see from this drawing that it's a simple outline drawing and it is basically a few distant hills, a middle distant pine forest, a lake and reflections with a few posts thrown in to take us into the distance. I want the sky on this one to be slightly brighter and more summery, a bit more warmth to the sky. I've got my board on a 45° angle, as usual, and I'm soaking the whole thing from the top of the paper to the horizon line with water and I'm going through the hills. Once all this is wet I'm mopping up surplus water at the base of the hills and my first colour is going to be a tiny touch of Burnt Sienna, well watered down, in the bottom areas. Whilst this is still damp I'm putting a little across the top line. I've got a mixture of French Ultramarine Blue with a touch of Alizarin Crimson mixed in with it; not enough Alizarin Crimson to make it go purple but just to warm up that blue a little bit and that's going all the way across the top line and letting the colours all run into each other. With my big wash brush, as normal I'm cleaning the wash brush out, squeezing out surplus water and taking out some big fluffy clouds. Now with a mixture of French Ultramarine Blue and a tiny touch of Light Red, well watered down, I'm just dropping this colour into the base of the clouds. At this stage I'm just softening that dark colour a little bit so it merges into the white bits of the clouds and there we have a fairly warm, summery type sky.

In the next picture you will see that I've filled in the distant hills and the key colour system applies again here. The distant hills have been painted with a mixture of French Ultramarine Blue with a tiny touch of Alizarin Crimson into it. Once this paint is on the hills and I've filled them all in, I'm now dropping in a tiny touch of well watered down Burnt Sienna and letting that merge into the hills a little bit; and just as in the previous painting, with a slightly damp wash brush I'm just sculpting those hills by taking out a little bit of paint with my damp brush.

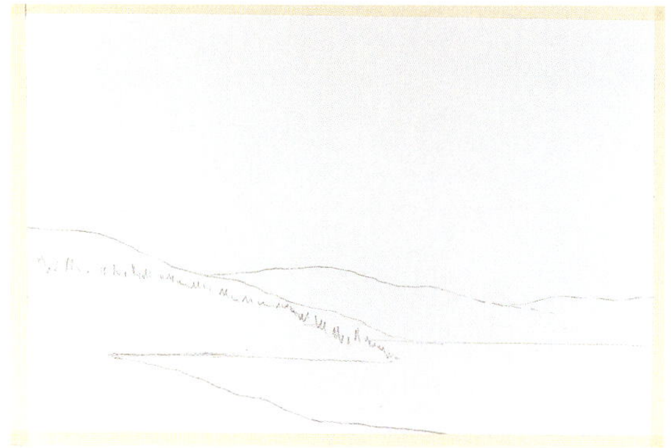

Outline Drawing

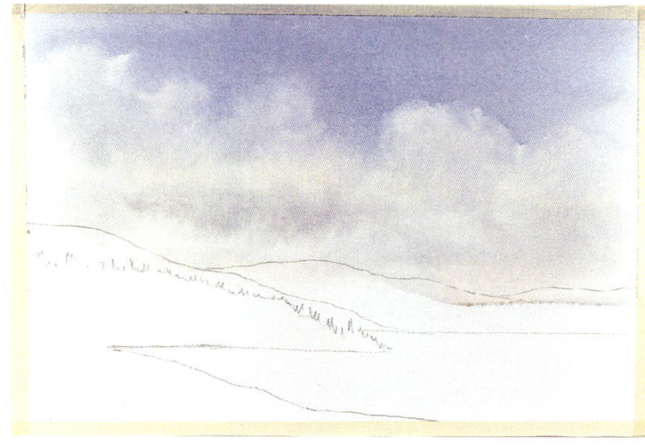

Warm Summery Sky

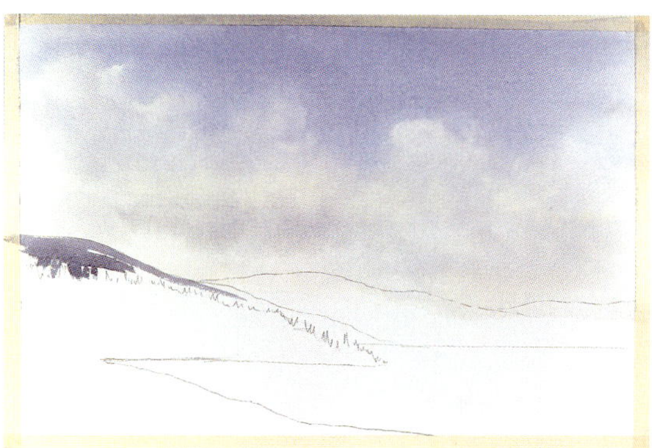

Distant Hills – French Ultramarine Blue with Alizarin Crimson

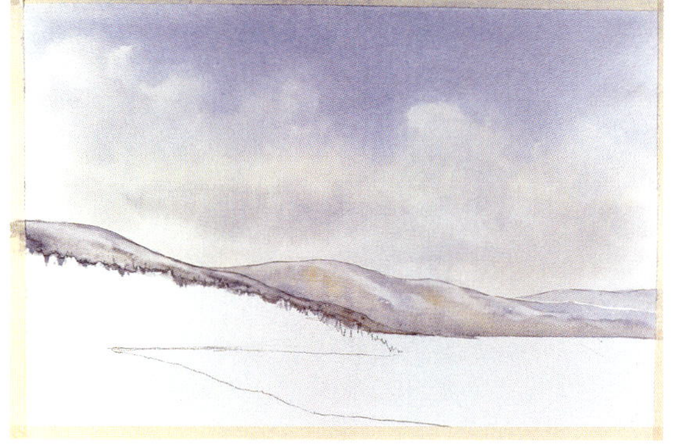

Distant Trees – adding Burnt Sienna

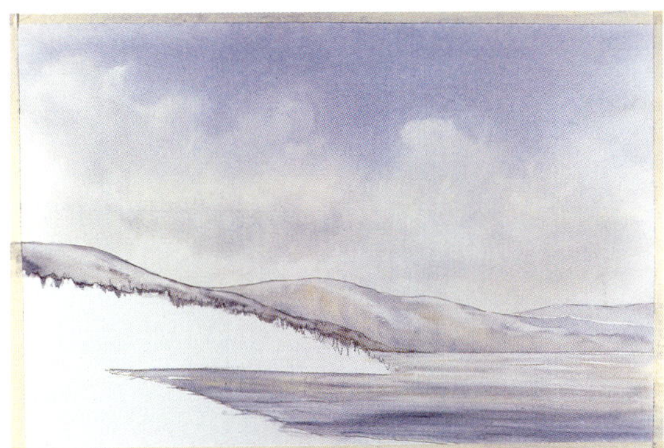

Painting the Water

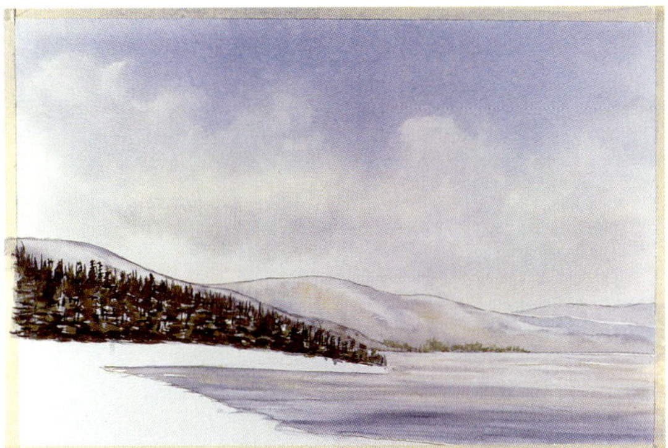

Distant Trees

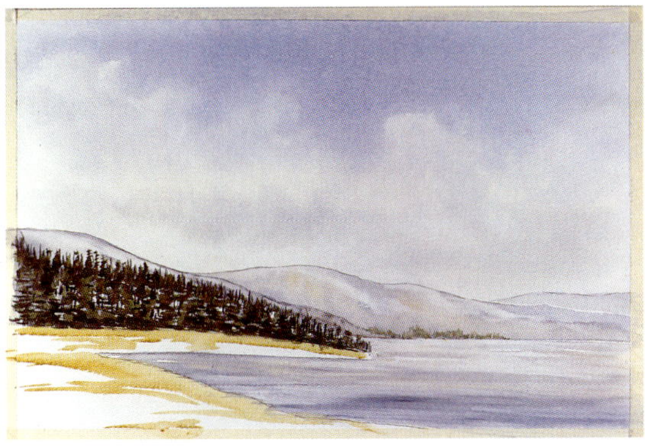

Grasses with Yellow Ochre

AS YOU will see in the next photograph, the next stage of this painting is the water. It is basically a repeat of the sky; the main colour being French Ultramarine Blue with a tiny touch of Alizarin Crimson in the blue, not enough to make it go purple but just to warm up the blue a little bit. I'm doing a large wash throughout the whole of the water area. Whilst my water is still damp I'm dropping in a tiny touch of well watered down Burnt Sienna and I'm letting this go throughout the blue and mingle in a little bit. Now with my cleaned out wash brush I'm just sucking out a few horizontal lines of paint out of the water area. This gives the effect of light catching the water and also with my rough surface water colour paper there are a few sparkly white bits showing through the water.

The distant trees on either side of the water have now been blocked in, in exactly the same way as I showed you how to do a distant pine forest in the small demonstration previously. A mixture of French Ultramarine Blue with a tiny touch of Alizarin Crimson being the key colour, to blot in the distant part of the tree poles. Then French Ultramarine Blue with a tiny touch of Burnt Sienna to slightly darken the blue is used to paint a few of the tree poles in front of the bluer ones. Now with my Hookers Green Dark and Burnt Sienna I'm doing a few horizontal strokes from side to side across the poles which makes it look like a distant or middle distant pine forest. A little bit of shadow colour is used i.e. French Ultramarine Blue with a touch of Burnt Sienna, just to darken underneath the trees a little bit and stroked down to form a shadow where the trees meet the ground underneath.

For my grasses around the water's edge I'm firstly going in with a touch of Yellow Ochre, well watered down, in the more distant areas of the grass, underneath the trees and around the middle distant areas.

IN THIS next picture you will see that I've now filled in all of the grass areas using a mixture of Hookers Green Dark with a touch of Burnt Sienna, well watered down, and this is a very loose wash to fill in that whole area.

In the next picture, once my grasses have dried, I've now gone in with a mixture of French Ultramarine Blue with a tiny touch of Alizarin Crimson into it and stroked over in different areas around the grasses to create some shadow and texture to the grass areas. The poles which I have put into the grass areas are now filled in with a mixture of French Ultramarine Blue and Burnt Sienna. Just straight poles at different angles which run from the grass area into the water getting progressively smaller as they go out into the water. This colour is repeated as reflection underneath the poles that are standing in the water, also repeating rough shapes of the trees in the water to form reflections.

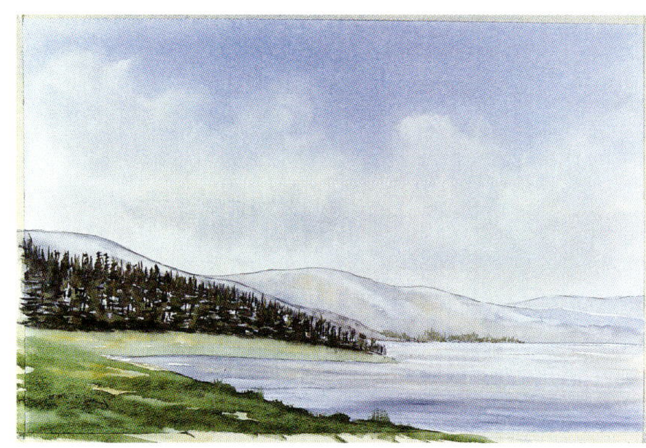

Filling in the Grass areas

Now with a very well watered down mixture of French Ultramarine Blue and the tiniest touch of Burnt Sienna, I'm stroking a few dark wash strokes into the already dried water to form some depth and darkness into the water as reflection and shadow. And there, that's another painting finished. Again not too difficult but slightly more difficult than the first one as we progressively build upon washes and more intricacies are added by the use of trees, reflection and shadows.

Adding Shadow, Texture and Poles

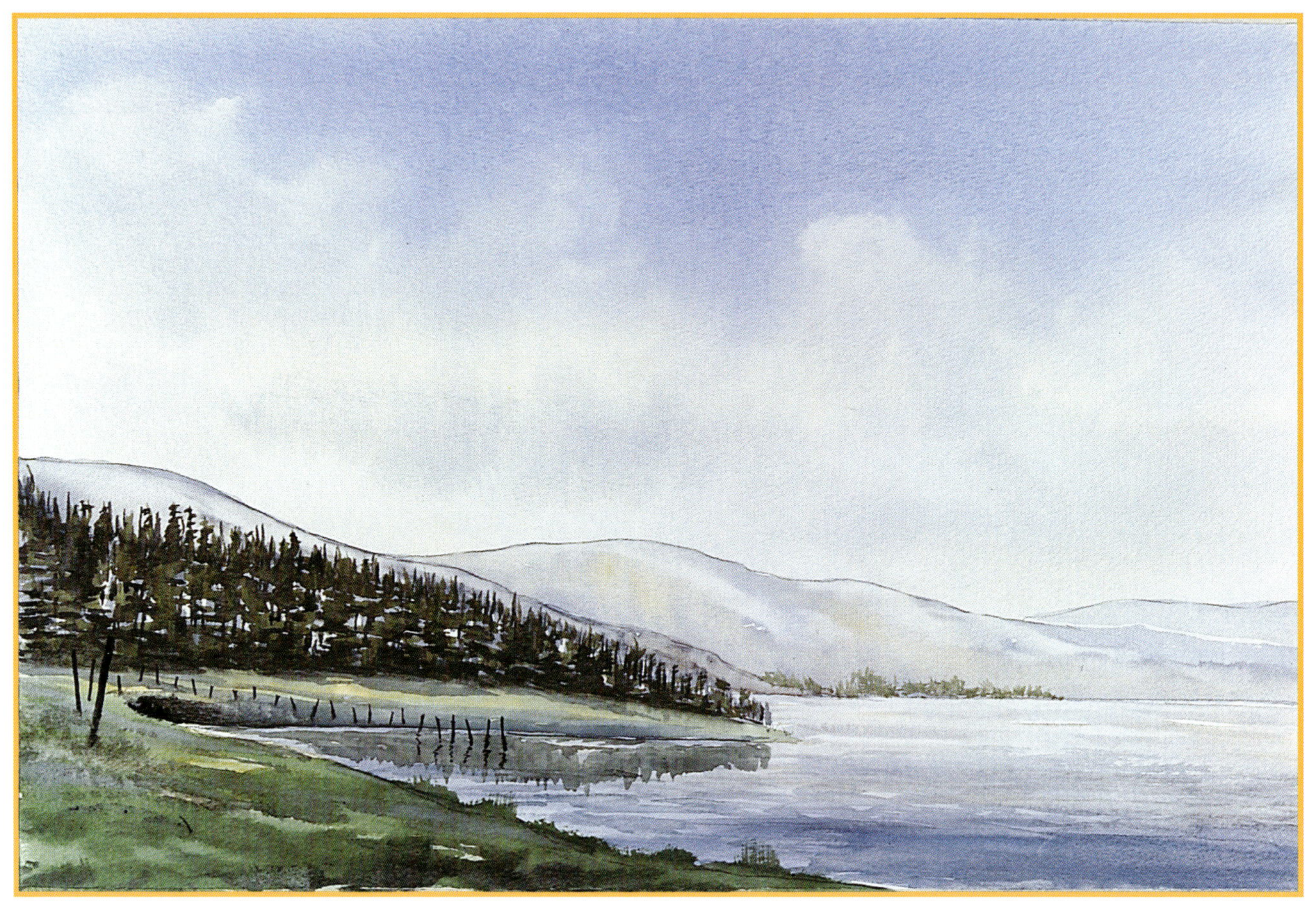

French Ultramarine Blue and Yellow Ochre Sky

Trees

Techniques, with & without Foliage

BEFORE we go onto the next type of tree, here's a little tip on how to get the effect of very, very distant trees on the horizon. In this first picture you'll see a very simple sky using French Ultramarine Blue and a tiny touch of Yellow Ochre.

Now in the next photograph you'll see that I have distant trees on the horizon line. This is done merely by dropping a mixture of French Ultramarine Blue with a tiny touch of Light Red, well watered, onto the horizon line whilst the sky is still damp. This makes use of the bleeding in process. Bleeding in is normally one of the hazards of watercolour painting because this happens when you don't wait for the first wash to dry before applying the next wash; but in this way it can be useful and we will be using this little tip in the next painting.

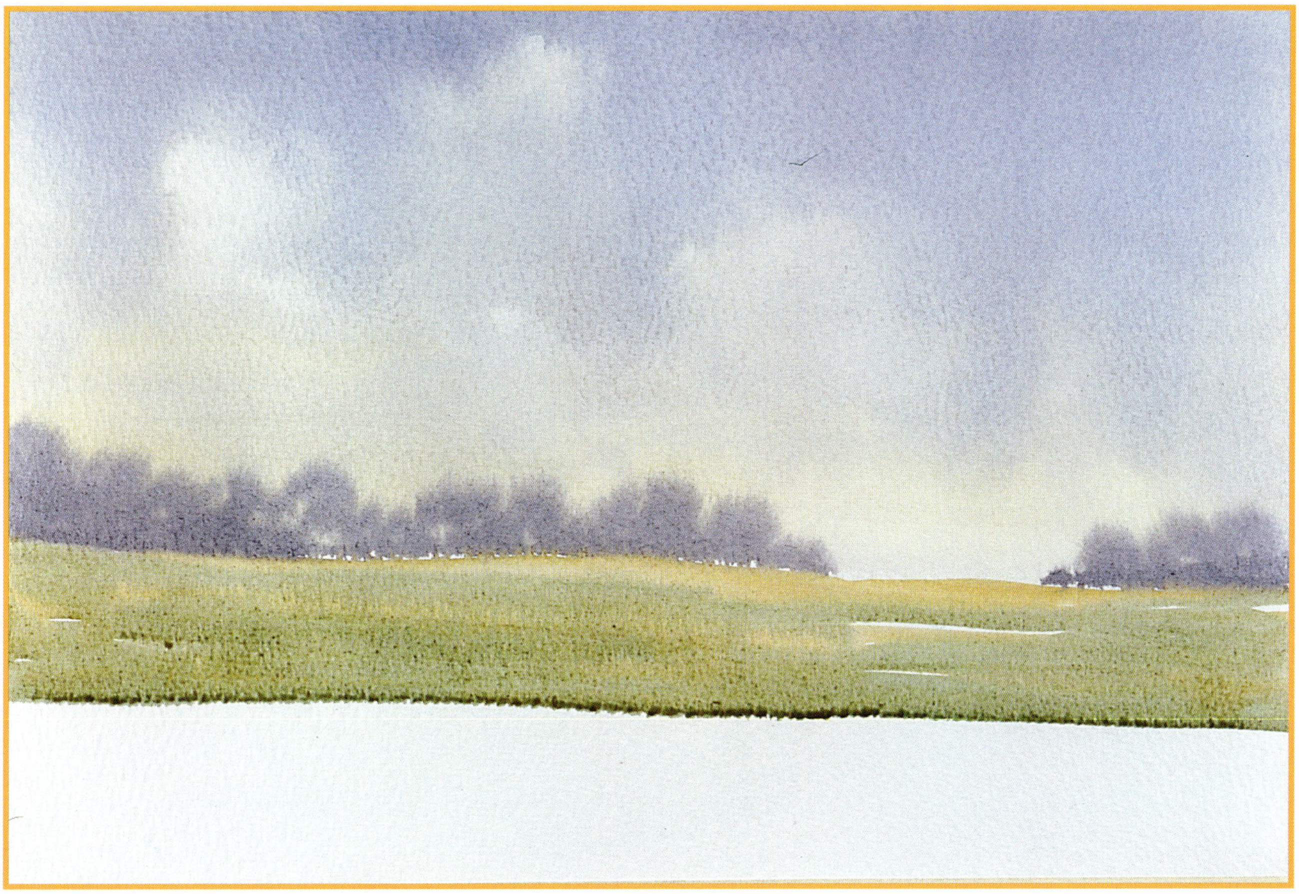

French Ultramarine Blue and Light Red Trees

BUT FIRST I'd like to show you how to paint trees both with foliage and without foliage. In this first picture you'll see that I've drawn in pencil the rough outline of a standard deciduous tree. It's not always necessary to draw the trees in pencil first but until you gather confidence in the painting of trees it's always useful to map out where you're going to make your marks. Using a size 6 round brush I've painted up the right hand side of the tree with a well watered down mixture of Yellow Ochre. Notice at this stage that I haven't gone into fine twigs with this mixture, I've just done the trunk and some of the bigger boughs towards the top.

In the next picture you'll see that I've filled in the other side of the boughs and the tree trunk with well watered, Raw Umber.

In the next picture, using a rigger brush, I've painted some of the fine twigs towards the top of the tree.

The next stage, as you'll see, is using the rigger brush to paint the extreme left hand side of the tree using a mixture of French Ultramarine Blue and Burnt Sienna which is very dark. To give the idea of a bit of roughness and texture to the trunk of the tree I just use this dark colour to flick across the main parts of the trunk using the side of the rigger brush. At the same time I've painted more fine twigs in this mixture of French Ultramarine Blue and Burnt Sienna. This gives the impression of fine twigs and a general rough feel to the top of the tree. I've put that into context with a bit of grass at the base of the tree, as if the tree is growing up out of the grass. There you have a fairly non-complicated tree without foliage.

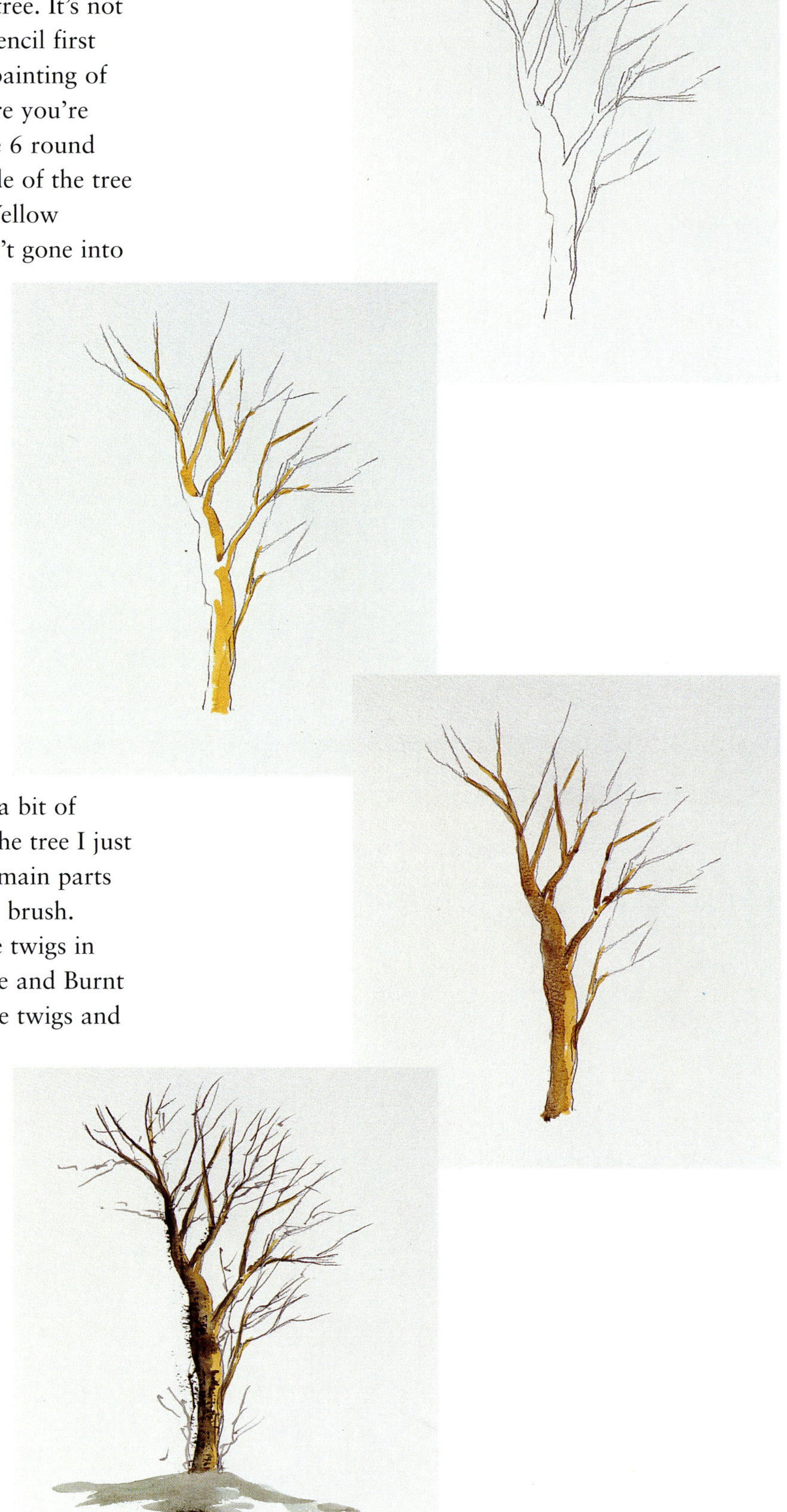

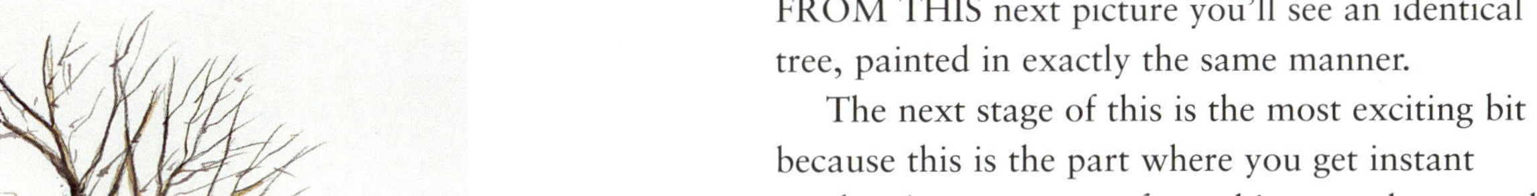

FROM THIS next picture you'll see an identical tree, painted in exactly the same manner.

The next stage of this is the most exciting bit because this is the part where you get instant results. As you can see from this next photograph I've washed in using my 1" wash brush with a little bit of Yellow Ochre in the top part of the foliage. At this stage I'd say yet again don't mess about with a small brush – use your wash brush. This makes it easier and the whole thing is more spontaneous.

In the next photograph you'll see that I've gone in with a mixture of Hookers Green Dark with a touch of Burnt Sienna and gone underneath the Yellow Ochre areas with this green creating my foliage. Remember to always leave gaps in the trees, you should be able to see some light through the foliage. Otherwise you could end up with lollipops on sticks.

In the next photograph you'll see the final tree. Again I've used my French Ultramarine Blue and Burnt Sienna mixture, really quite dark, and gone underneath the main areas of foliage with my shadow colour. This is creating some shadow underneath the foliage and also onto the trunk so that the foliage is casting shadow onto the trunk. Now put the whole thing into context with a swathe of grass underneath the tree and it looks like we've got a full blown tree in foliage.

Painting – *Snow Scene*

FOR THE next painting I want to paint a snow scene and will be utilising the trees without foliage, both distant and foreground. Snow scenes are usually very effective paintings with the minimum of effort and we can get a very pleasing result with a big broad wash painting. But don't forget, as you'll learn in this painting, snow is not always white.

You'll see from this outline drawing that I've roughly drawn in a foreground tree, a slightly further away tree, some middle distance trees and some very, very distant trees and I've marked out the area where I want to give the inclination of a path. As you can see from this drawing, we'll be using the method I showed you for doing very distant trees, and the method I showed you for doing the trees without foliage. One close up, as in the demonstration, another one practically identical but weaker and further away.

A good tip on how to get the effect of a snow scene is to have the light snow against a fairly strong sky. That doesn't necessarily mean a dark sky but if it's going to be a blue sky have it a bright blue sky. This is known as counter-change, the dark colour against the light colour and is usually a very effective way of achieving a pleasing result. The sky wash in this photograph has been done by wetting the paper thoroughly, all the way down to the horizon line, and then going into the bottom areas with a touch of Yellow Ochre well watered down. Above this I leave a gap for my cloud areas and in the top of the paper I put French Ultramarine Blue with the tiniest little touch of Alizarin Crimson, not enough to make it go purple but just enough to warm the blue up a little bit. A huge swathe of that across the top and let it run down. I then wash out my large wash brush, dry it out and then with circular scrubbing motions suck out some of the paint from the paper to create my clouds. Now with a mixture of French Ultramarine Blue and a touch of Light Red I put this into the bottom area of the cloud whilst the paper is still damp and just let it soften into the bottom parts of the clouds; this is creating the base of the cloud, the shadow if you like.

In this picture you'll see that whilst my sky is still slightly damp with my mixture of French Ultramarine Blue and Light Red I touch into the bottom areas on the horizon line with my mixture of paint well watered down and just let this seep up into the sky ever so slightly so that I get the distant hazy effects of very distant trees. Now I let the whole thing dry before I go onto the next stage.

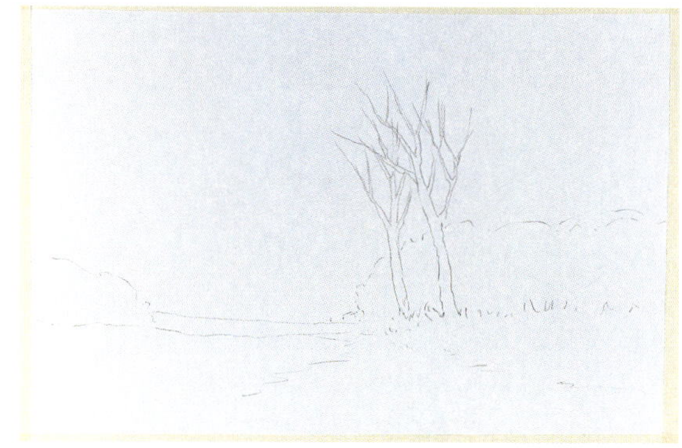

Outline Drawing

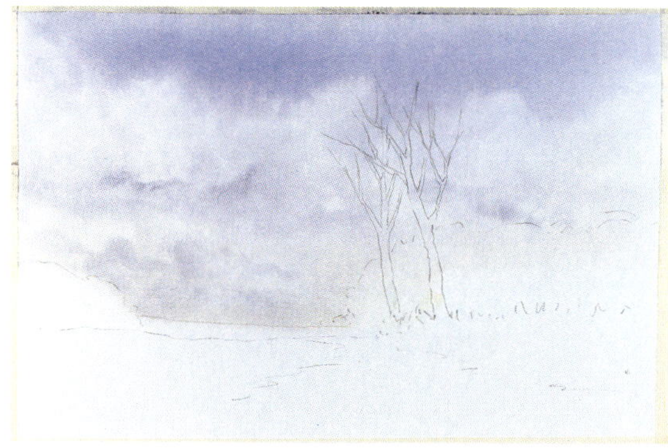

Strong Blue Sky

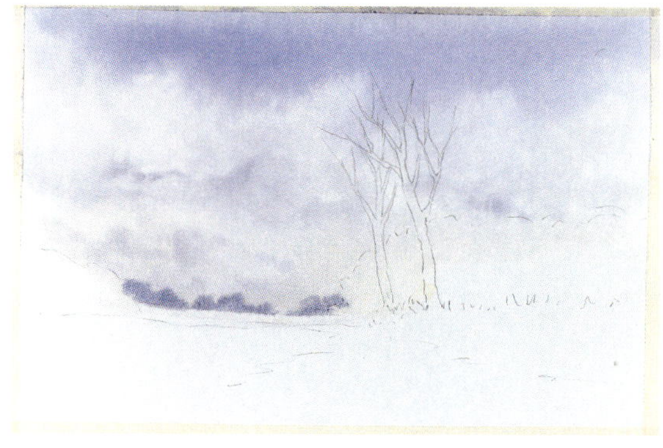

Distant Trees

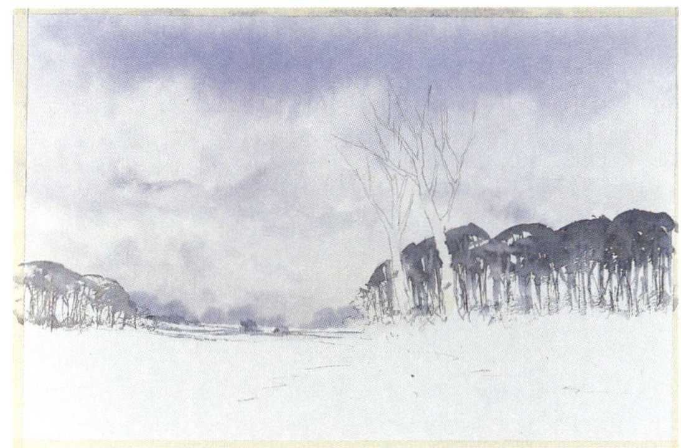

Middle Distance Trees

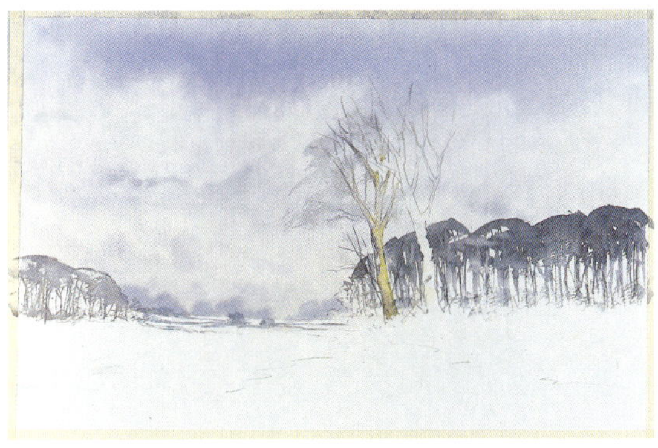

Main Trees – Yellow Ochre

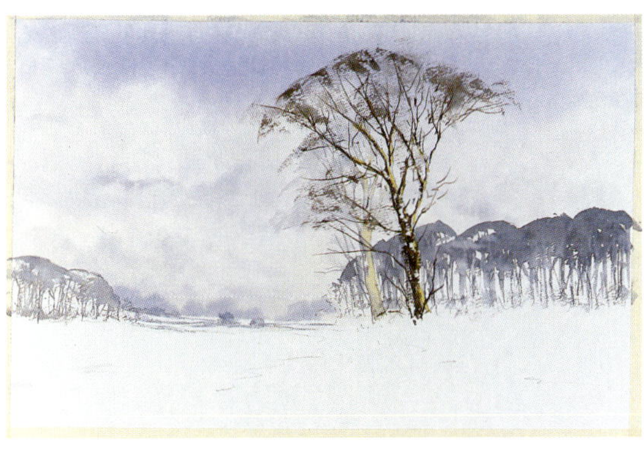

Adding French Ultramarine Blue and Burnt Sienna

THE NEXT stage of this painting is to fill in my middle distance trees and for this I use my mixture of French Ultramarine Blue and Light Red, very well watered down and with a very small round brush I paint in the trees I have already drawn. This is fairly easy method of doing it because all I'm doing is really filling in the areas that I've already drawn. For these trees I don't go to town with the twigs because at the distant I want these trees to appear you wouldn't see so many fine twigs individually marked out on the tree. Once I've painted the amount of trunks and boughs and the small amount of twigs that I want I then, clean out my brush, dry the brush and then dip into the already mixed paint of French Ultramarine Blue and Light Red and with a dry brush, stroke over the canopy of the tree. This gives the effect not of foliage but dry, scratchy looking twigs in the top areas of the trees. Whilst I have this mixture of paint, French Ultramarine Blue and Light Red, with the tip of my round middle sized brush I dip into the well watered paint and do a few horizontal strokes across the middle distant areas of the painting, coming up to the base of the middle distant trees. This gives the effect of the snow lying on the ground but not too detailed because it's middle distance.

Now for the furthest away of the two main trees in the painting. This is a stage when I want to start to add a little bit of light into the painting and what better place to capture the light than on the trunks and twigs of the trees. So here you'll see that I've painted this tree using firstly Yellow Ochre on the right hand side of the trunk. This is a very well watered down Yellow Ochre so it's really quite weak, and just a stroke of the colour up the right hand side and into the main boughs and a few of the twigs.

While this is still drying using a mixture of French Ultramarine Blue with a tiny touch of Burnt Sienna I go up the left hand side of the tree in a similar manner, painting the main trunk, few of the boughs and a few of the twigs but keeping to the left side of the tree.

My next stage is to strengthen this mixture of French Ultramarine Blue and Burnt Sienna and do a line up on the left hand side of the tree, sticking really to the edge of the tree and painting a few of the twigs in this same colour. It is interesting to note not to get the French Ultramarine Blue and Burnt Sienna mixture too dark. It wants to be a dark colour but not too dark because otherwise the tree will come too far forward in the painting and vie for the position with the main tree in the foreground. Again the final stage of this tree is to use my dry brushstrokes of French Ultramarine Blue and Light Red in the top areas, creating a bit of canopy of twigs.

AS YOU'LL see from this next photograph the main tree in the painting now dominates everything else in the view. This is painted in much the same manner as the one behind it but the colours are all a little darker with the addition of one extra colour. You'll see that I've painted on the right hand side again with Yellow Ochre to capture the light and the feel of light coming from the right had side of the picture, then up the central parts of the tree I paint Raw Umber, fairly well watered down Raw Umber and that's just sticking to the central bits of the tree and up into the boughs and the twigs. Then again on the left hand side I use my French Ultramarine Blue and Burnt Sienna mixture, first fairly well watered down and then stronger sticking to the left hand side and going up with a fine line and into the twigs. All this is done whilst the first colour is still slightly damp. This way I get a feel of the colours running into each other and I don't create some kind of a colour sandwich instead of a tree trunk. Now using my rigger brush, still with French Ultramarine Blue and Burnt Sienna, I scrape at the side of the tree on the left hand side giving the feel of a few bits of rough bark and growth on the sides of the tree. You'll also note from this photograph that I actually paint in more twigs using my rigger brush with the French Ultramarine Blue and Burnt Sienna because, don't forget, this tree is a lot closer, you can see more detail in the tree and so I need to see more twigs. So I paint in a lot of twigs and then the final stage is still with my French Ultramarine Blue and Burnt Sienna mixture to do a very dry rough brush stroke, breaking up the paint and this gives the feel of rough texture to the top of the tree but it's also darker than any of the other trees.

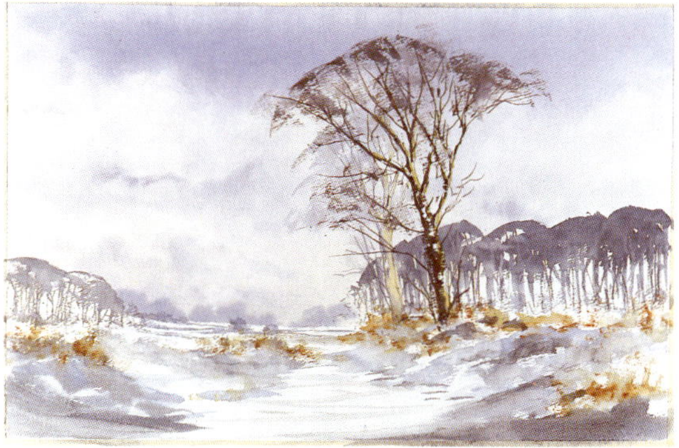

Rough Growth – Yellow Ochre

And now it's time to get to ground level but before we paint the snow we'll paint the growth and using a size 8 round brush I dip, with my dry brush, into a ready mixed Yellow Ochre, well watered down, and using the side of my round brush I do quick upward stroking movements with the dry brush. This gives a rough growth effect coming out of the ground and I also repeat this with the same strength of Burnt Sienna, just here and there along the bottom areas of the trees and the edges of where the path is going to be.

And now to the snow. At this stage I'll tell you that if you were to leave just a vast area of white paper showing, which believe me I've seen done often, then it really wouldn't look like snow, it would look like a piece of white paper left unpainted. So we have to give some texture and movement to the snow and give some undulation to the ground. For this I've used a mixture of French Ultramarine Blue with a touch of Light Red, darker in the foreground

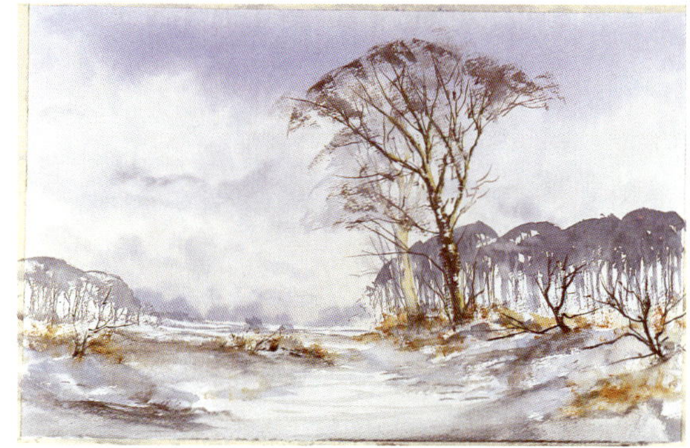

Snow – French Ultramarine Blue and Light Red

and then adding more water as I get further away into the distance to join up with the middle distance areas which we painted earlier. Then just using touches of French Ultramarine Blue by itself and fairly strong I add some shadows into the more foreground areas and the edges of the path. I then go back to my French Ultramarine Blue and Burnt Sienna mixture and put a few dry brush strokes here and there to represent some bits of rough stuff coming up from underneath the snow. I also put a few strokes into the path to signify a few lines, cracks and probably even hidden stones with just the tops peeping out underneath the snow.

And as you'll see in the finished picture the last stage is to add my posts and this is quite important because again it gives a feeling of distance to the painting. All are done in French Ultramarine Blue and Burnt Sienna and notice I haven't kept any of them straight, they're wiggling about at all different angles. The only important thing to remember is that they get smaller as they go further into the distance. Once I've painted each post I then, with my sharp edged small 1⁄2" flat brush, suck out a little bit of paint from the right hand side of each post giving a feel of light to one side and dark to the other side. And there we have yet another finished painting.

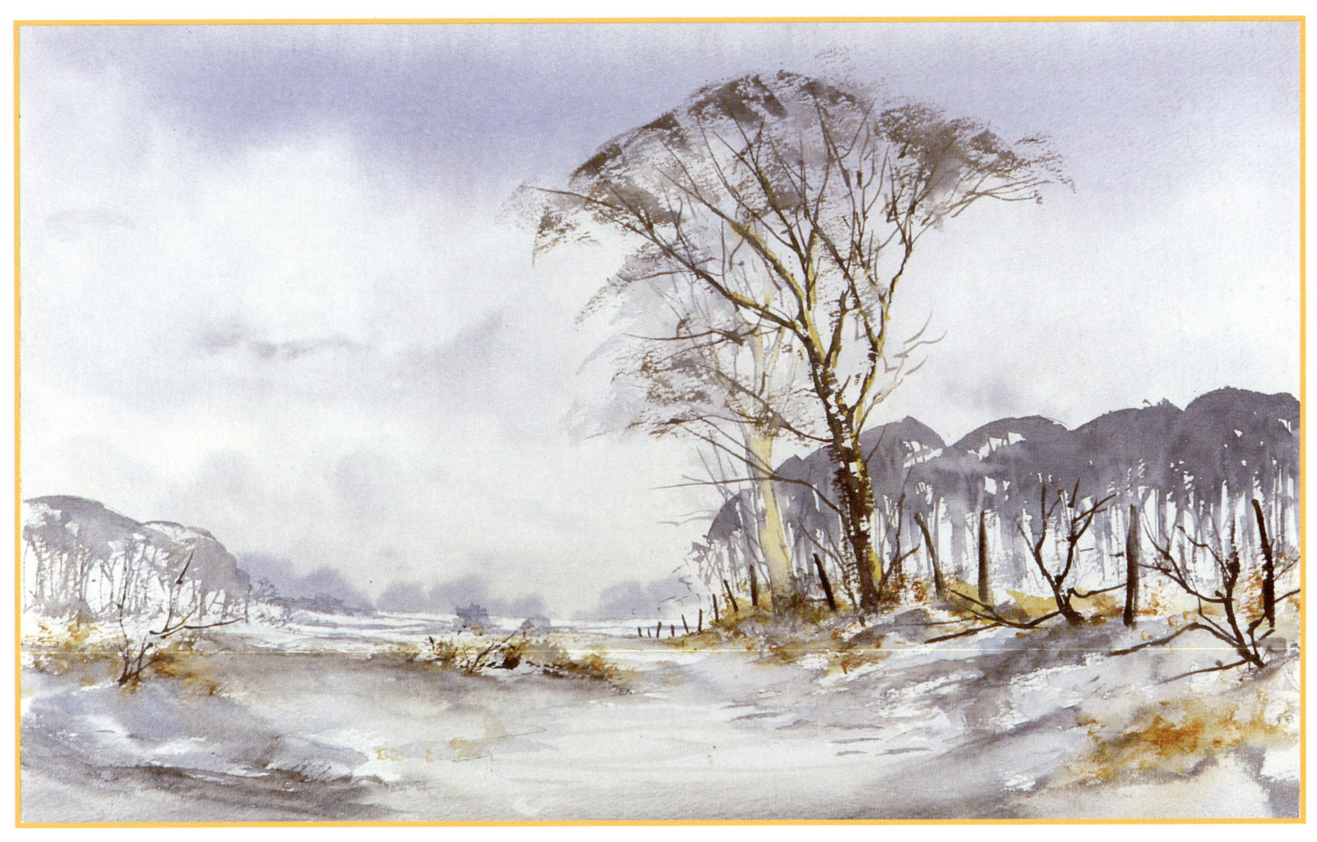

People & Animals

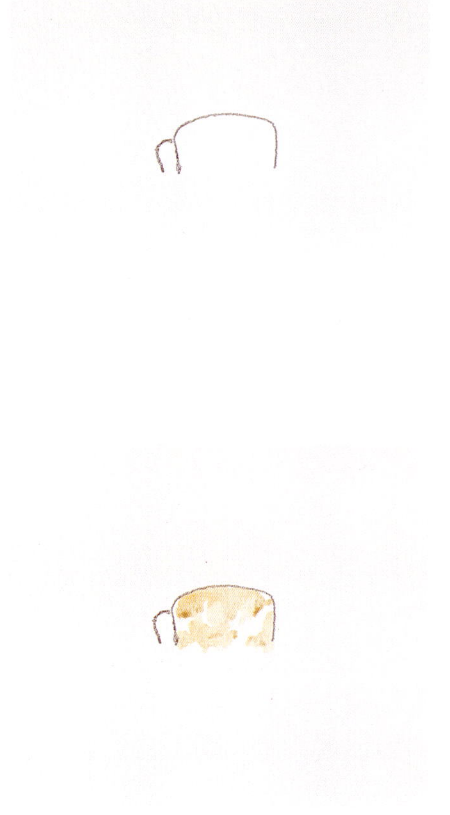

BEFORE we go onto the next painting I'd like to show you how to introduce a bit of life into a painting. What better way to introduce life than putting either people or farm animals into your landscape and for this example I'll be showing you how to paint a few people and sheep. Now at this stage you're probably thinking to yourself "oh my god I can't do this", but don't worry, sheep are not as difficult as they sound. And as you'll see from this photograph the drawing really looks like a loaf of bread with a little lump on the end and that's all you need. Don't start painting or drawing legs and ears and heads and tails and all the rest of the complicated detailed things which end up making your paintings look far too fussy and busy, just stick to the loaf of bread with a little lump on the end.

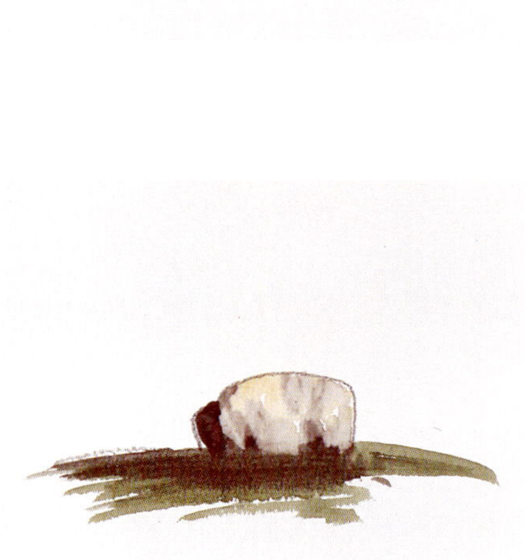

Now you'll see that the next stage is to paint the top area of my loaf of bread with a well watered down Yellow Ochre. Then whilst the Yellow Ochre is still damp, using a small brush, I just paint a mixture of French Ultramarine Blue and Light Red to represent where the legs would be and give the impression of a roundness of the back, just stroking into the Yellow Ochre allowing the two colours to mingle in a little bit together.
Once this is dry the next stage is to paint the head using a mixture of French Ultramarine Blue and Burnt Sienna, very, very strong, almost black and just paint the little lump on the end of the loaf of bread. Once it is dry add in strokes underneath with a little green to make it look as if it is standing on the grass.
A stroke of shadow using French Ultramarine Blue and Burnt Sienna, well watered down, and hey presto there's your sheep standing grazing.

AND NOW onto people – the nightmare of most painters work. You'll see from the next stages, I don't do any drawing first for the simple reason that if you draw your people first then paint on top, sticking to the lines of the drawing, you end up with very stiff motionless figures instead of spontaneous movement. You'll see from the first picture I've just done two dots – two round dots, one lower than the other and this is done using French Ultramarine blue and a touch of Burnt Sienna, but not too dark.

Now first with the left hand figure, doing the body first with well watered down Yellow Ochre and using a small pointed brush I merely block in an area with Yellow Ochre and give the impression of a couple of arms. Then I go back to my French Ultramarine Blue and Burnt Sienna mixture and start off at the base of my Yellow Ochre area, the same width of the base of the Yellow Ochre area and painting downwards to bring it to a fine point where the figure will touch the ground. For the figure next to this one I have done it in exactly the same manner but for the body part I've used Alizarin Crimson and for the legs the same mixture of French Ultramarine Blue and Burnt Sienna. Now in the context of a landscape these two figures will look like a pair of people walking away in the middle distance. You could even outstretch the arms so that they meet in the middle and then the couple will be walking away hand-in-hand.

As you will see from these next figures, I've painted them in exactly the same manner but weakened the colours considerably and also a couple of the figures I've done in purely French Ultramarine Blue with a tiny touch of Light Red, well watered down, and this makes the figures go even further away so they're very much in the distance.

I once did a painting for Tyne Tees Television which was the Great North Walk and I stood in a position overlooking Durham Cathedral with thousands of people walking past me at great speed on a sponsored walk. Now probably only the first six or eight figures were actually painted in different colours. The rest were in varying degrees of strength of French Ultramarine Blue and Light Red or French Ultramarine Blue and Burnt Sienna and this gave the impression of people in the foreground and the rest were just a backdrop of people going away from me. I think you'll find that this is a very effective way of getting some life and movement into your painting. It also focuses the eye on a central part of the painting.

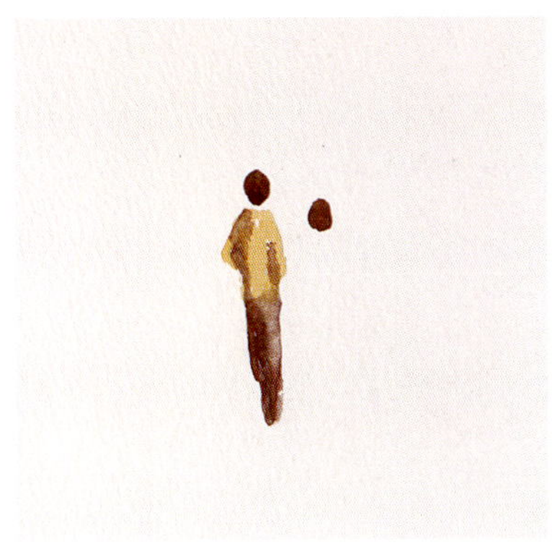

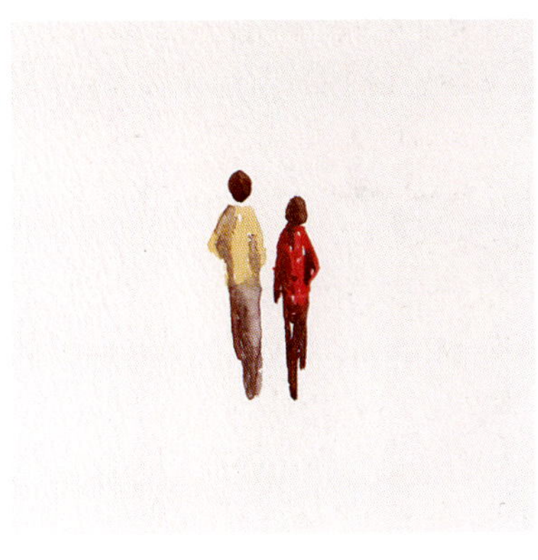

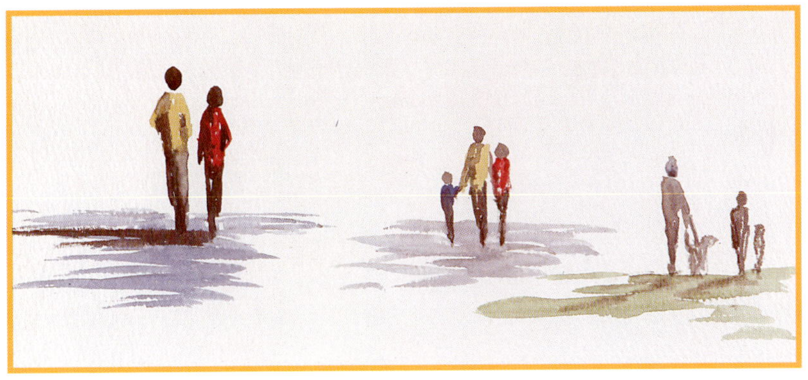

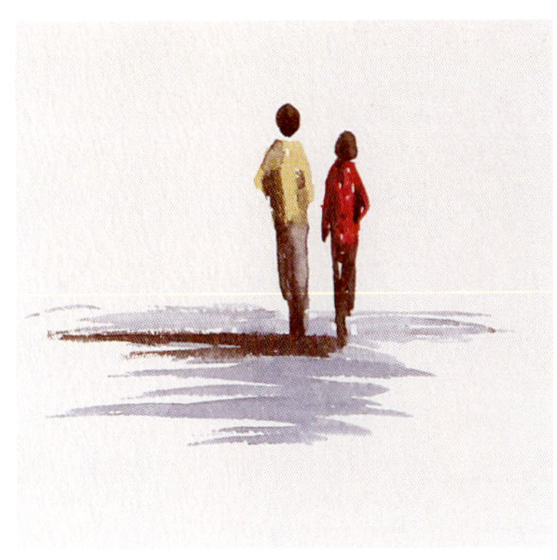

Painting – *Autumn Scene*

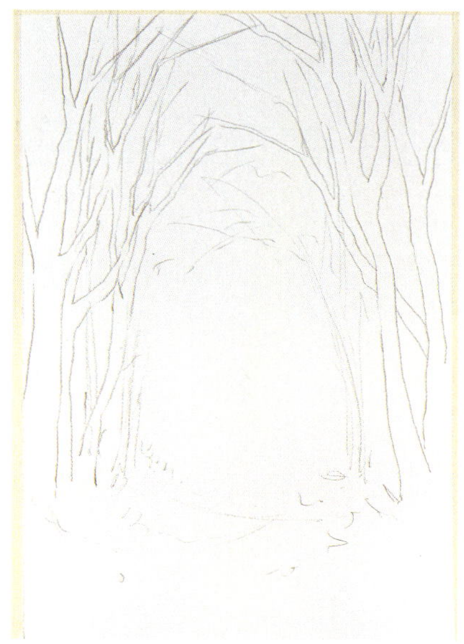

AND SO let's move on to the next painting. And for this we're going to have a tree lined lane with middle distance people walking away form us and this is going to be a lovely autumnal scene. As you'll see from my drawing, there are quite a lot of trees in this painting but the foreground trees, down to about three trees into the distance, are the only ones that are really quite detailed with quite a lot of twigs and boughs hanging over to form a lovely archway. As the trees get more distant there's less and less detail in, so that eventually in the distance they become just poles going off and getting smaller. You'll note at this stage that I haven't drawn the people in because, as I said, these people are just going to be almost an afterthought in the distance walking away and that will be sufficient to add the life. So don't draw them first.

In this next photograph you'll see that the sky is already painted and there's no need to mess about or be too fussy with this sky. It's just literally a well watered down mixture of French Ultramarine Blue with plenty of water and just stroked down, going through the trees and everywhere. Because, don't forget, you're not going to see much of this sky – there's just going to be glimpses of it through the trees.

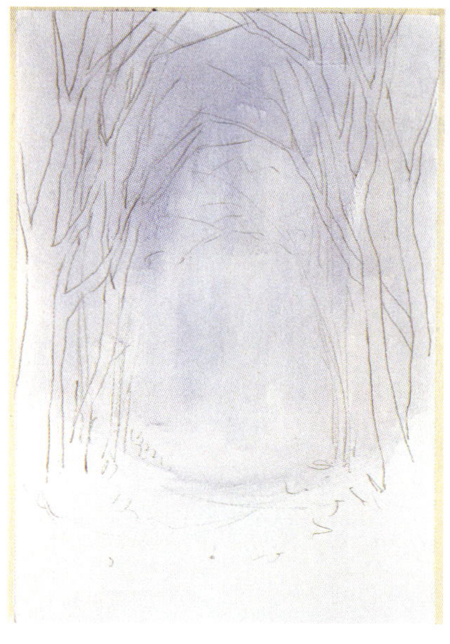

In this photograph you'll see that nearly all my distant trees are completed and I do it whilst the sky is still ever so slightly damp, not so damp that the trees will fade into the sky, but just to give that little touch of moistness at the edges of the trees. This I achieve by using French Ultramarine Blue with a tiny touch of Burnt Sienna mixed into it and just do them very simply blocked in with a medium sized round brush until I get to the last three of four trees either side of the pathway. You'll see in the next picture I've painted in Raw Umber, just block them in with the same medium size round brush and don't pay too much attention to detail.

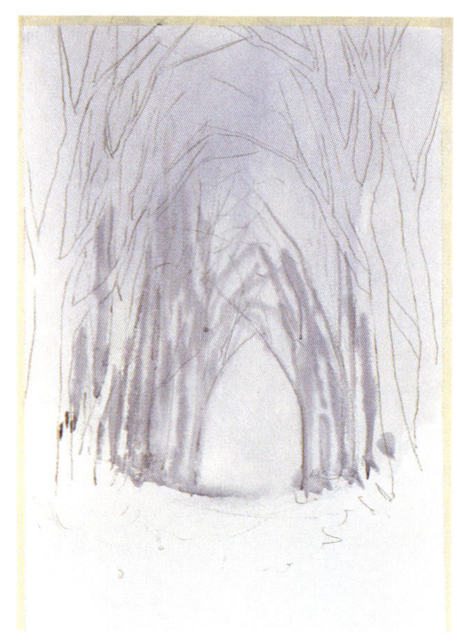

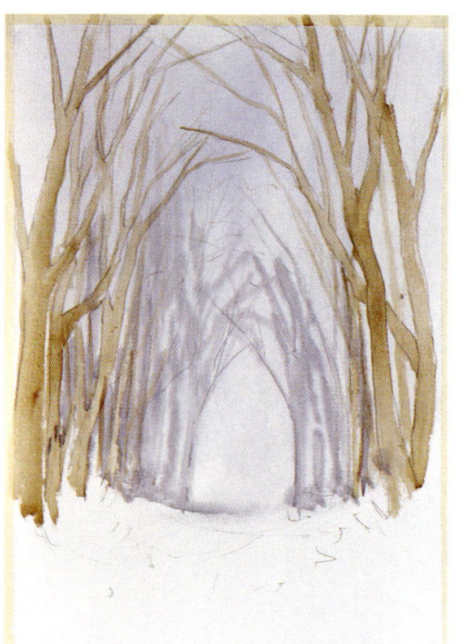

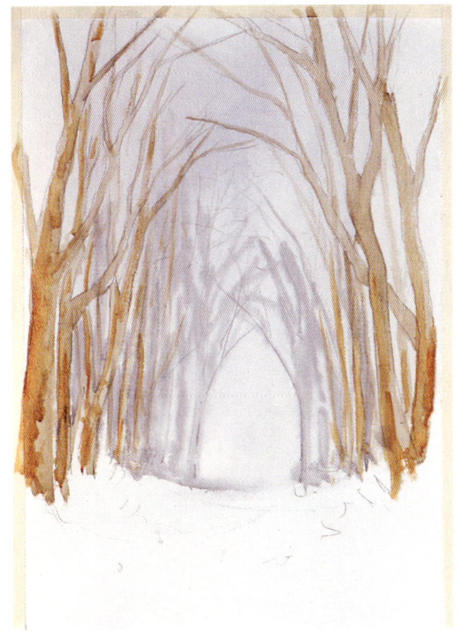

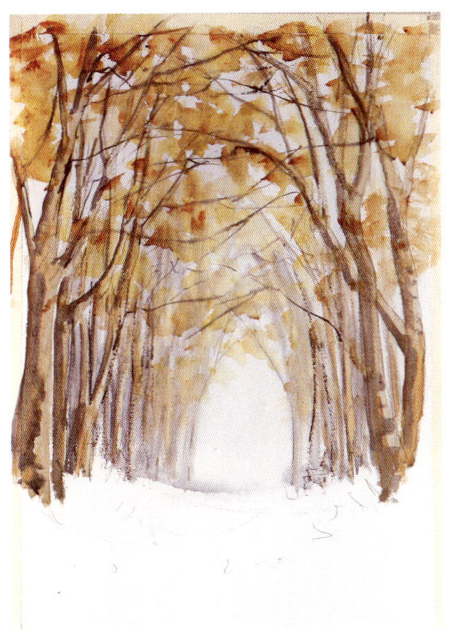

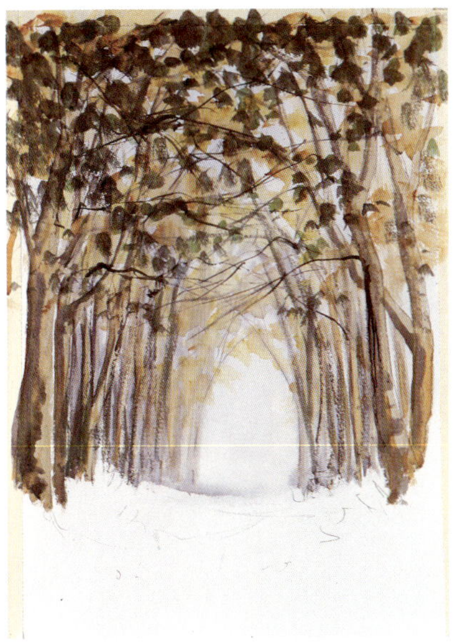

IN THIS next picture you'll see that I also add some Burnt Sienna into the Raw Umber whilst the first colour is still wet. Also at the left hand side of each tree I put a mixture of French Ultramarine Blue and Burnt Sienna covering about a third of the width of each trunk and taken that all the way up in the top of the trees where I've also painted some twigs in the same colour. Now you see in this picture the foliage in the distance is painted in Yellow Ochre and whilst this is still wet dab on some well watered down Burnt Sienna, all whilst the first colour is still wet. Just liberally daub these colours in the distant areas forming this archway of foliage until we get further into the foreground where I strengthen my colours slightly.

The foreground here is painted in the same two colours, Burnt Sienna and Yellow Ochre but with the addition of a mixture of French Ultramarine Blue and Light Red. This I build up really quite strong in the foreground so that you're looking through a darker archway of foliage off into the distance. Then with the rigger brush and a mixture of French Ultramarine Blue and Burnt Sienna I paint fine twigs coming down and out of the archways creating individual tipped twigs which make the painting look more three dimensional. You have the hard edged twigs in front of you looking off into the distance.

Now with my No.10 round brush I've got a mixture of Hookers Green Dark, French Ultramarine Blue and Burnt Sienna to form a very dark, rich green – very very dark. I dab the colour on with the point of my round brush and eventually the brush will form itself to create a leaf shape. This I'm just dabbing here and there creating a few individual leaves in the foreground trees.

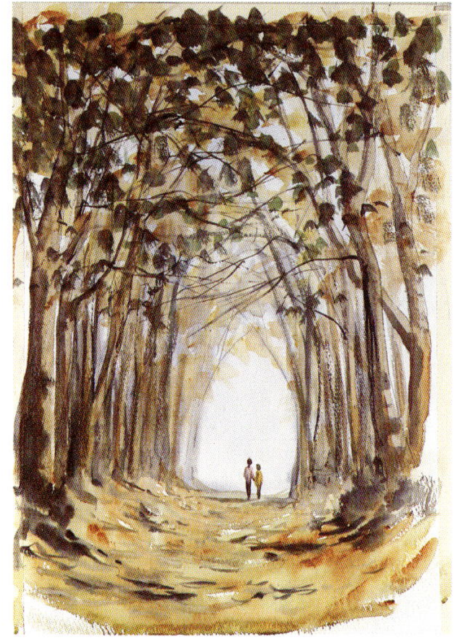

THE NEXT stage is to form the path and in a curving motion I paint Yellow Ochre, well washed down, all the way down the path off into the distance. Whilst this is still very, very damp I use Burnt Sienna, well watered down, and just dab on here and there to create warmer patches in the path which will also represent fallen leaves. In a similar way I also dab on a mixture of French Ultramarine Blue and Light Red, just here and there, and also painted a few strokes of this in the same curling motion into the path, backwards and forwards in an arching motion of the brush. As you'll see here I've actually painted the people in now and remember there was no drawing first, in exactly the same way as I showed you earlier. And here is the finished picture. As you'll see I've now put in the final shadows, painted in a very dark mixture of French Ultramarine Blue and Burnt Sienna in the foreground, getting weaker as it goes off into the distance. Remember, shadows get weaker as much as any other colour gets weaker. Notice the way the shadows cast from the trees fill up a great deal of the path, leaving just shafts of the original yellow and Burnt Sienna colour showing through as if the light is shining through the trees and dappling on the pathway. And there we go, another painting bites the dust.

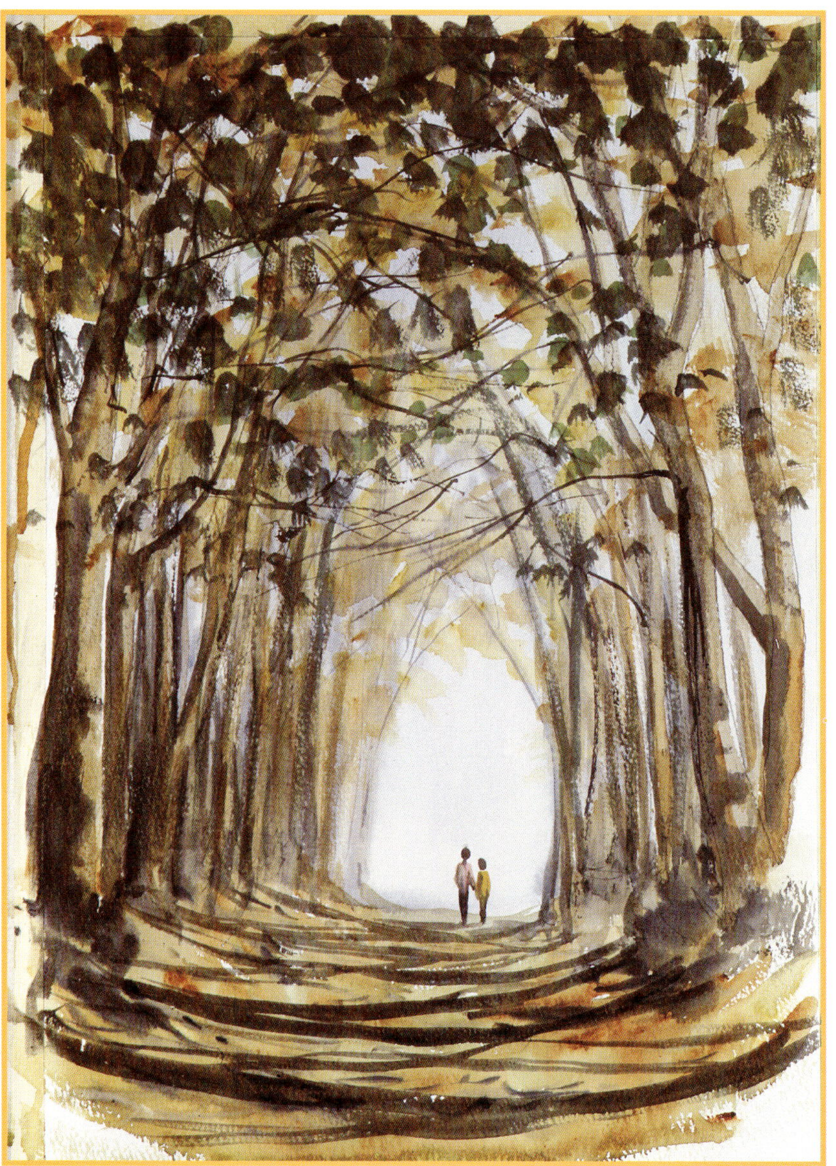

Houses

I NOW want to introduce some buildings into my landscapes and so before we go on to buildings here's a little bit about perspective and vanishing points. But don't worry I'm not going to go into too much detail and I'm not here to try and confuse you with technical terms. But just take a look at these two drawings. The first drawing is of a small moorland cottage and the second drawing is exactly the same moorland cottage with the vanishing points drawn on. You can see how the roof of the building goes away from us by falling off in a diagonal way as much as the base of the building goes upwards in a diagonal way. This is creating, if you were to draw a line along the roof of the building and a line along the bottom of the building out into the distance, your vanishing point. Also note on the drawings how simple and uncomplicated both the chimneys and the windows are. In the context of a broad landscape on any building you don't need to see net curtains and windows in the window frame. You just need to give the suggestion of a window; and the same can be said of the chimneys. But you'll also note that the top of the windows are also going away from us in that diagonal scope.

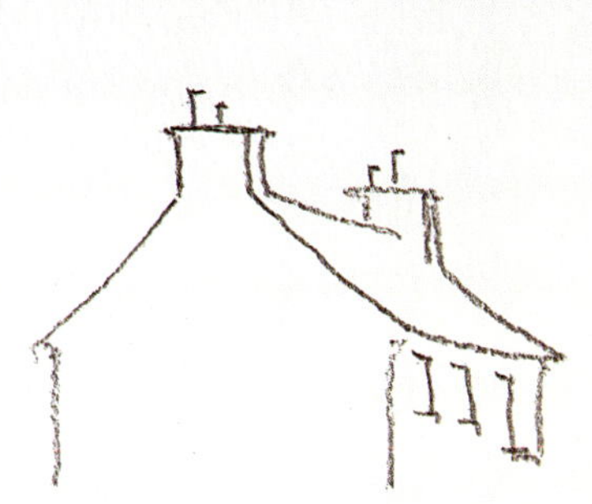

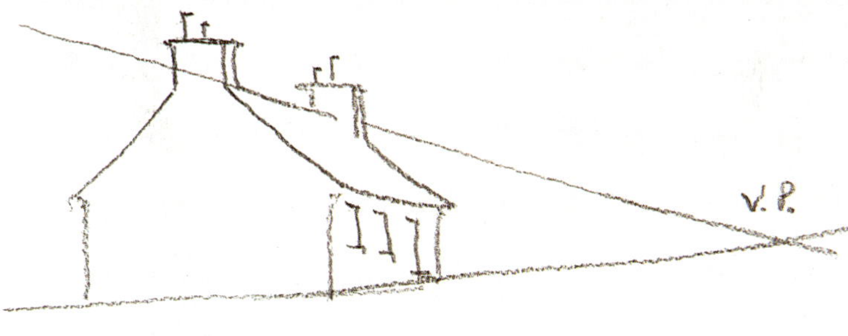

Painting

Moorland Cottage and Sheep

SO IF WE put this building in the context of the landscape, as in the drawing pictured here, you'll see that the building sits right in the landscape and actually looks as if it's larger at one end and smaller at the other end, thus creating the feeling of going away and vanishing points. You may also notice that in the landscape we're going to make use of one of my earlier demonstrations and that's sheep. We're going to put some sheep in our moorland scene.

And so on to the sky. With my board on a 45° angle and using my usual large wash brush, as you'll see in this picture, I have a fairly overcast sky. This I achieve by watering the paper down well and putting a tiny bit of Burnt Sienna in the bottom areas, broad strokes across the bottom area of the sky and a well washed mixture of Burnt Sienna. Above this I apply a well watered down Warm Sepia in a broad stroke straight across the middle section of the sky, then immediately above that I use French Ultramarine Blue with Burnt Sienna from the top coming down into the Warm Sepia and let those colours run in together. Then I wash my large wash brush out, squeeze out surplus water and I take out some fairly horizontal clouds, not big fluffy clouds this time, just a few indications of cracks of light coming through the sky.

In this picture you'll see that I've filled in the distant hills. There are two hills in all. One slightly weaker which is just French Ultramarine Blue on its own with plenty of water and the one in front of it French Ultramarine Blue with a touch of Burnt Sienna, so I am making it a little bit darker here. Then, with my washed out wash brush, I take out a little bit of the paint that I've already applied, sculpting those hills and giving them a bit of shape and movement.

You will see here that I fill in my middle distant areas next and for this I use a mixture of Yellow Ochre and French Ultramarine Blue to make fairly dull type of a green. I apply this colour whilst the base of my hills is still slightly damp. That way I'm not going to get a hard edge where the hills meet the middle distance, it's going to be slightly hazy and a bit damp looking. I apply the green and then take out little bits of colour with my large wash brush, just sucking out some of the colour to create a bit of light into the middle distance areas here and there.

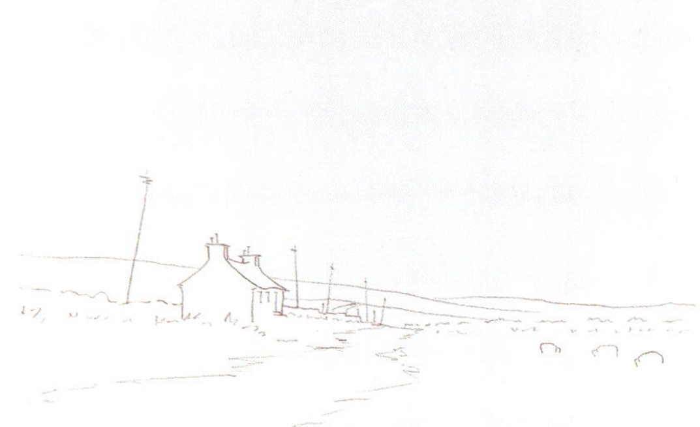

Moorland Cottage Drawing

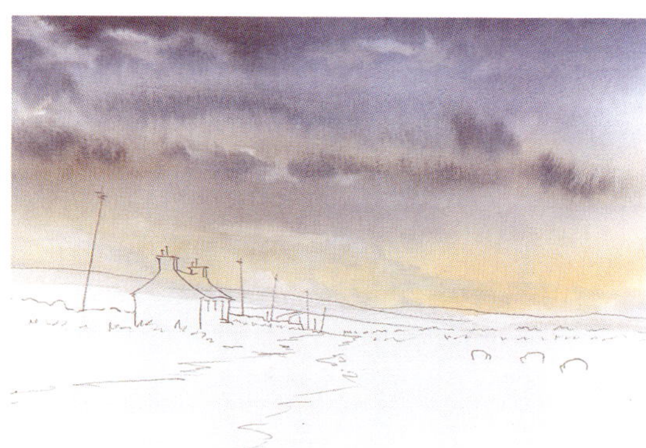

Overcast Sky

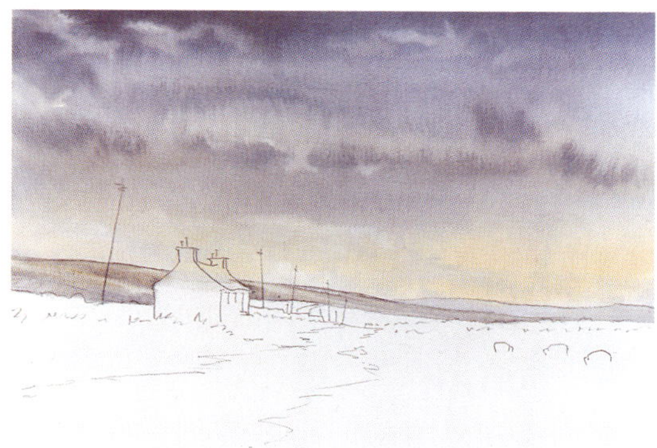

Filling in the two Distant Hills

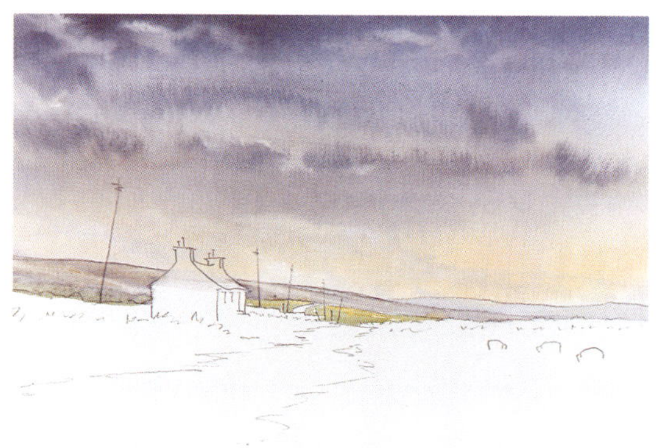

Middle / Distant Areas

HERE you'll see I wash in the whole of the cottage with a well watered down Raw Sienna; wash the whole thing, chimney stacks and both sides of the building and let this dry. At the same time I wash down the dry stone wall leading up to the cottage and coming out from the other side of the cottage with the same colour, Raw Sienna. Because, don't forget, on top of a moorland if you have a dry stone wall next to a cottage it's very likely that the wall is going to be made out of the same stone as the cottage, so keep the colours the same. Once the walls of the building are dry I then paint in the roof and for this I use French Ultramarine Blue with Light Red. A light wash first, and then once this has dried I darken the same colour slightly by using less water and put a few slicks of this dark colour into the pale colour of the roof. This gives the idea of the few rough tiles and lines in the roof.

The next stage of the building is to actually add a bit of texture and surface as if it's made of stone into the walls and for this I use Warm Sepia, fairly strong Warm Sepia, not too much water. I just kind of stipple the colour on with the tip of a round brush on the near side wall which is going to be the darkest part of the building. Also remember the far chimney of the building has also got a near side and a far side and so I stipple the Warm Sepia onto this as well. At the same time notice that I use the same technique on the dry stone wall. Here you'll see that I do a very haphazard wash of Yellow Ochre in the foreground grass areas but take great care to go around my loaves of bread which will eventually become sheep. Also, whilst the Yellow Ochre is still very wet, I drop into this some Burnt Sienna here and there just to warm up the scene a little bit. You'll see that I also paint the whole of the path with the Yellow Ochre, and I do this using fairly dry brush strokes to the path so that I'm leaving sparkly bits of my white rough surface paper showing through the Yellow Ochre.

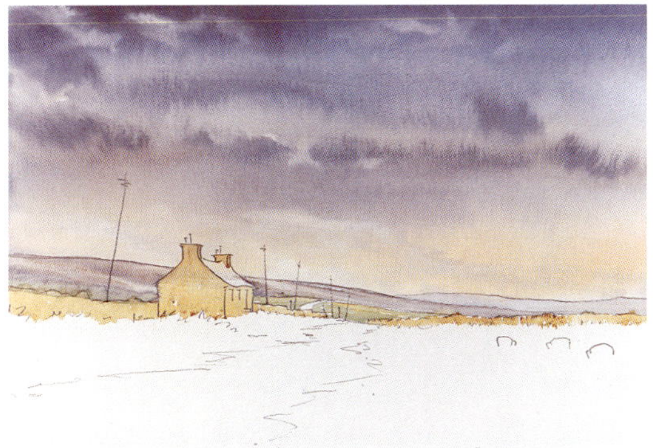

Adding the Cottage with Raw Sienna

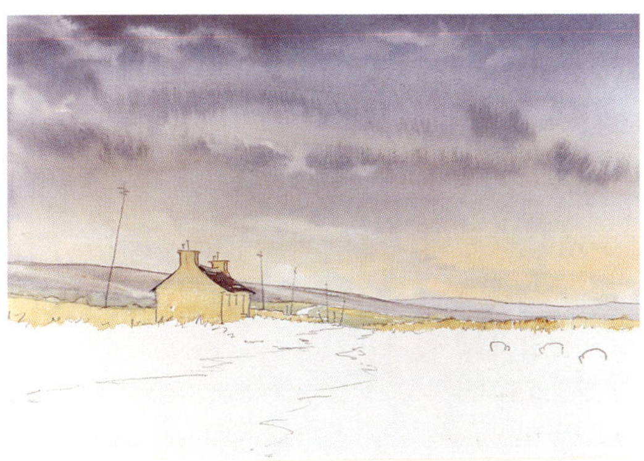

Paint in the Roof

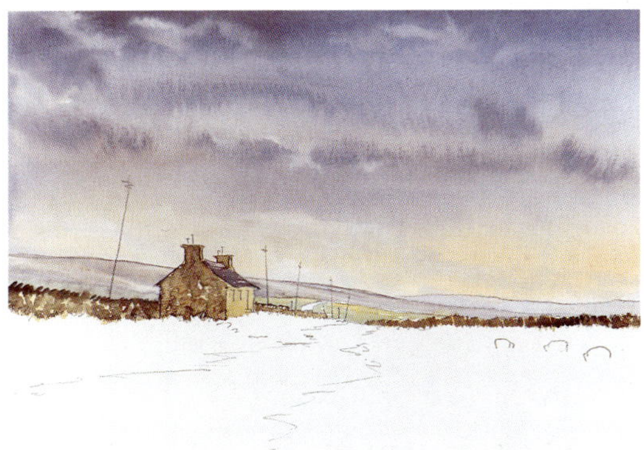

Adding Texture with Warm Sepia

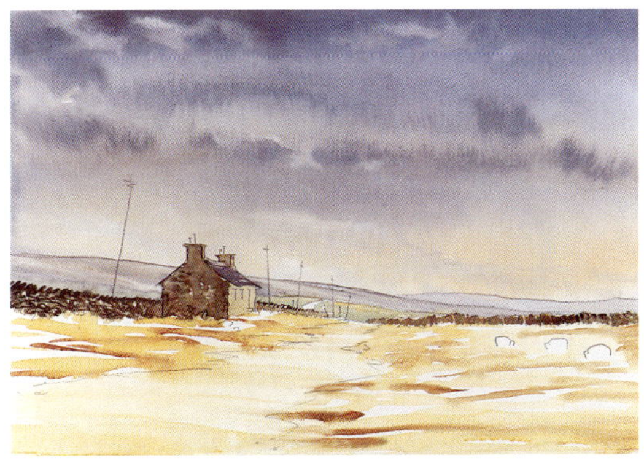

Foreground Grass and path with Yellow Ochre

THE NEXT stage is to add a mixture of Hookers Green Dark with Burnt Sienna, fairly strong, in amongst the Yellow Ochre and Burnt Sienna colours that I've already put on the grass areas. I'm still leaving a few little areas of the white paper showing through.

Now I go back to the building with a mixture of French Ultramarine Blue and Burnt Sienna and using dry brush strokes I just stroke over the already darkened areas of the building. Also with this colour I put a thick dark line underneath where the roof meets the building. This is forming a shadow cast by the roof onto the building. At the same time using the same colour mixture, French Ultramarine Blue and Burnt Sienna, I paint in my windowframes and my door, just as I showed in the previous demonstration, and also I paint the chimneys.

On top of the dry stone wall I put a few posts. Up on top of the moors these posts are normally on top of walls to hold wire mesh that runs at the top of the walls to stop the sheep from jumping over the dry stones. My finishing touch is to paint in the sheep, remembering to put in a little bit of shadow to make them look as if they're really standing in that long grass. Then, using dry brush stokes again go over the path, this time with a mixture of French Ultramarine Blue and Light Red, again leaving sparkles of the rough surface paper showing through, this time in white and the previous colour of Yellow Ochre. And there we go, here's our moorland scene with sheep and building. Now that wasn't too difficult was it?

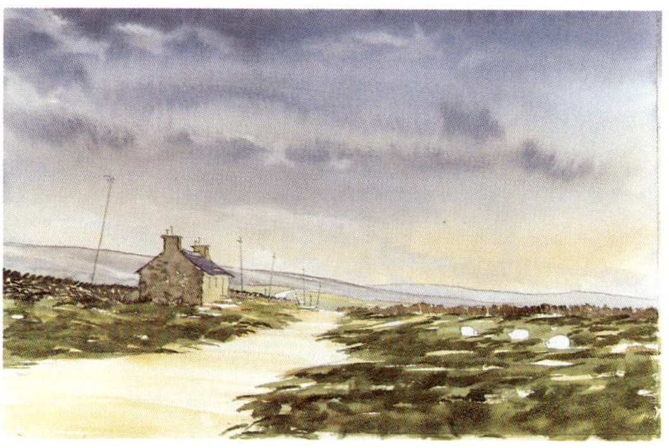

Adding Hookers Green Dark with Burnt Sienna to the Grass

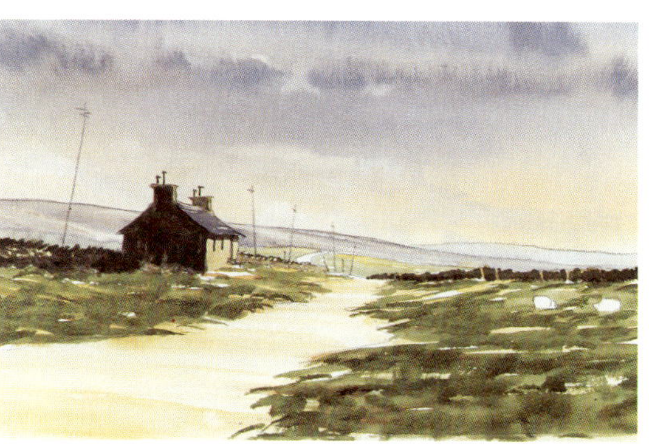

Back to the Building with French Ultramarine Blue and Burnt Sienna

A few Posts on the Dry Stone Wall

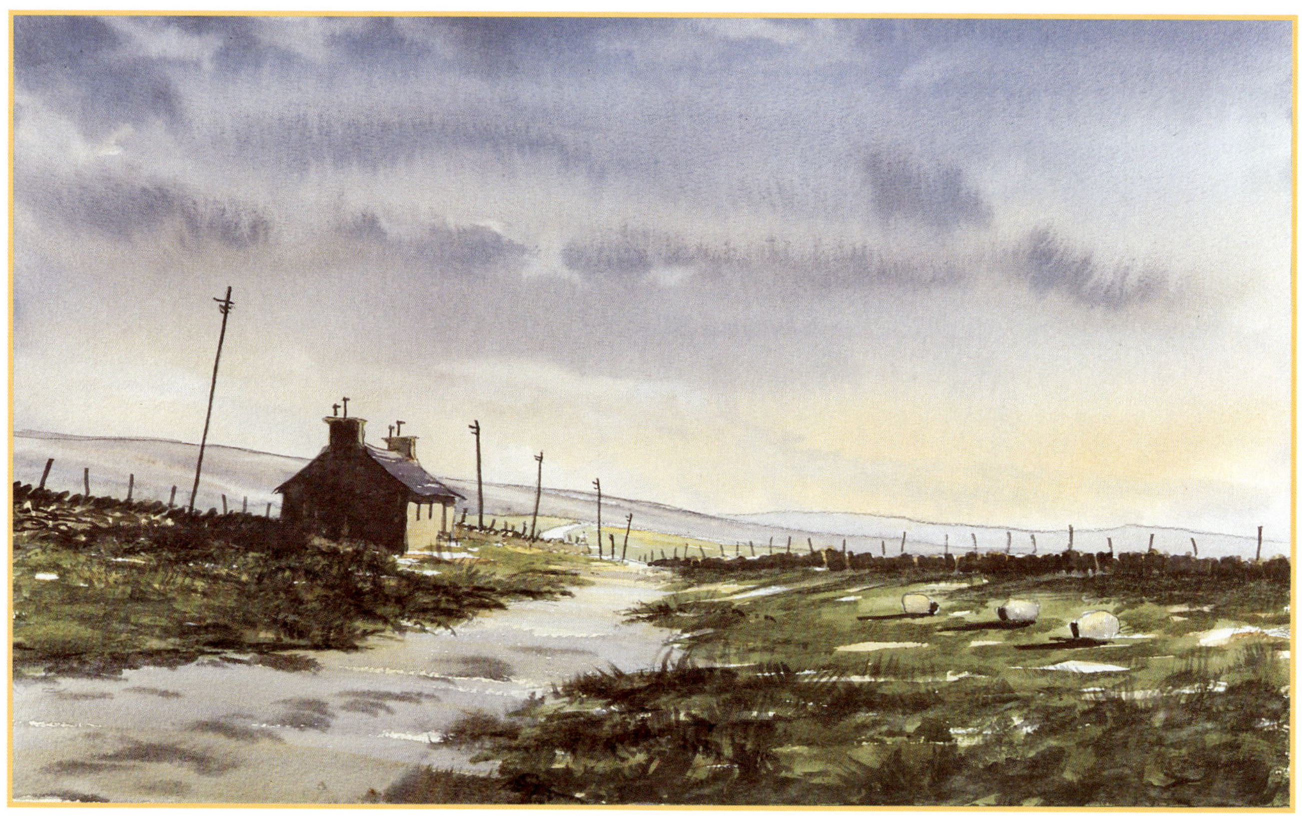

Ivy - *Buildings & Trees*

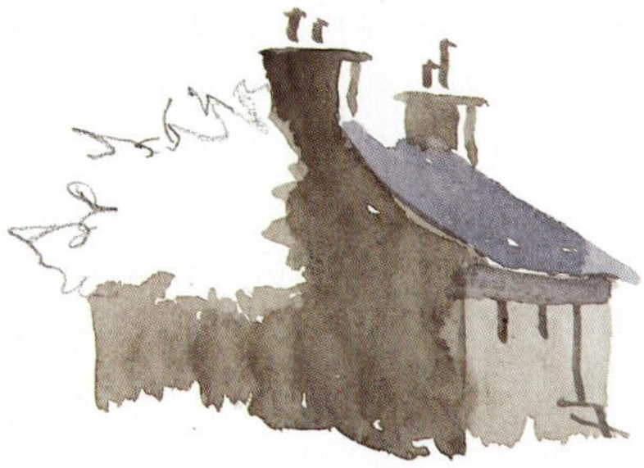

THE NEXT thing is something which is quite often seen as really quite difficult to paint and that is Ivy. Ivy growing up on buildings or on trees. This is the kind of thing that really adds quite a lot of interest to a painting but needn't be as difficult as it looks. I intend to simplify it for you so that you can use it in your painting.

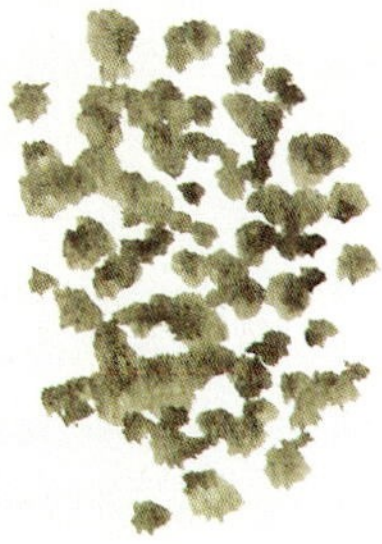

First we take a look at the partially done painting of the small cottage. Now this is exactly the same type of cottage that we've just done in the last painting, but you'll notice that I haven't painted in the area where I intend the Ivy to go. Instead all I do is with my pencil draw the rough area where I would like the ivy. Here is an example of the effect that we're after.

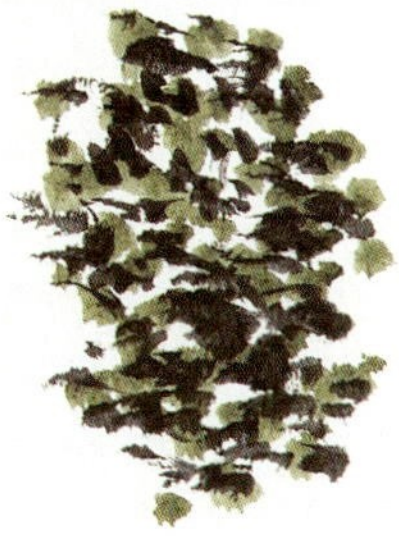

Now to achieve this effect I use my large round wash brush and with a mixture of Hookers Green Dark and Burnt Sienna, just stipple on leaving tiny speckles of white paper showing through. These small specks of white are very important because this is the only source of light that you're going to get into the Ivy so make sure you leave these. Now with a mixture of French Ultramarine Blue and Burnt Sienna, very very dark, in a similar manner I stipple on to the green so that this is showing shadow underneath the leaves of the Ivy and there, you have a fairly convincing clump of Ivy.

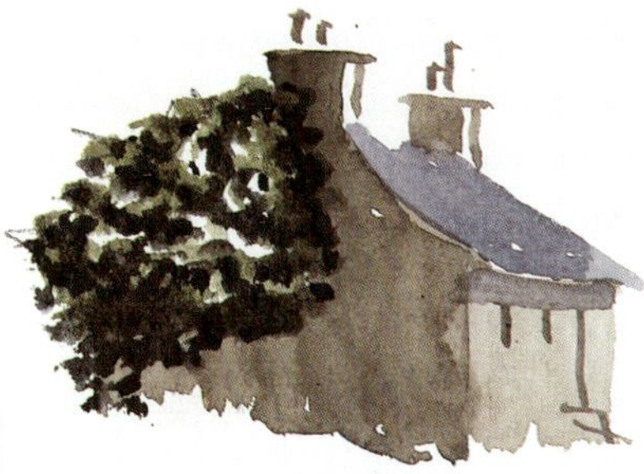

In this next picture you'll see that I've added that clump of Ivy to the side of the building and put a little bit of shadow where the Ivy actually touches the building. The shadow colour is painted in French Ultramarine Blue and Burnt Sienna. This just makes the whole thing just sit down on top of the building rather than look like it's perched on top of it.

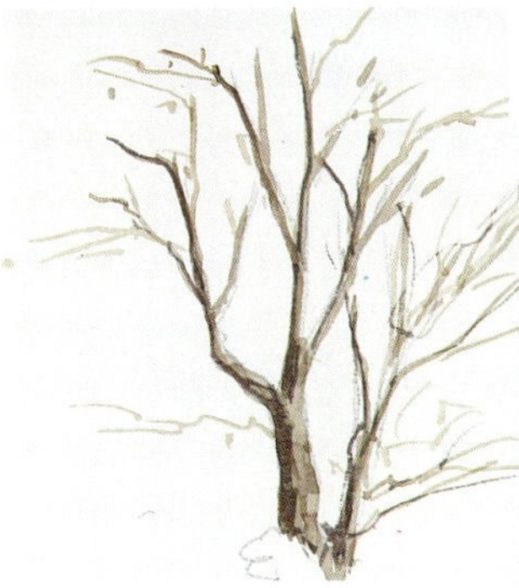

In this picture you'll see a partially painted tree. The tree is painted in exactly the same manner as I did in the demonstration on trees but I just leave out the areas where I'm going to paint the Ivy. Here you'll see I add the Ivy to the tree and it looks like an Ivy-clad tree, good and rough around the main trunk area with the addition of a few little twigs coming out of the Ivy itself. The twigs are painted using my rigger brush and with a mixture of French Ultramarine Blue and Burnt Sienna, very dark, just paint these growing out of the Ivy in all different directions.

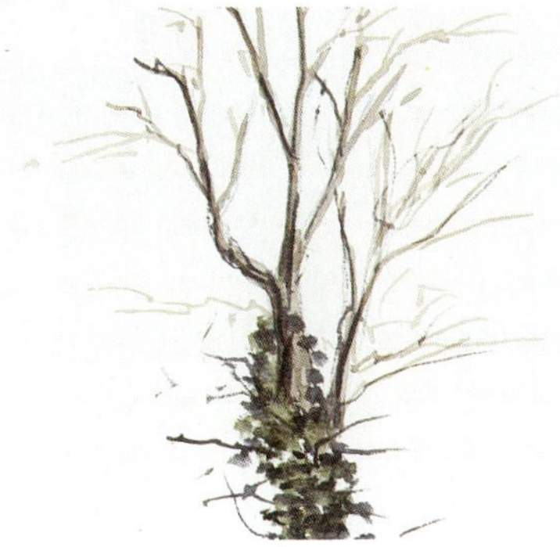

It's all these little touches that make the difference between a fair landscape painting and an excellent landscape painting.

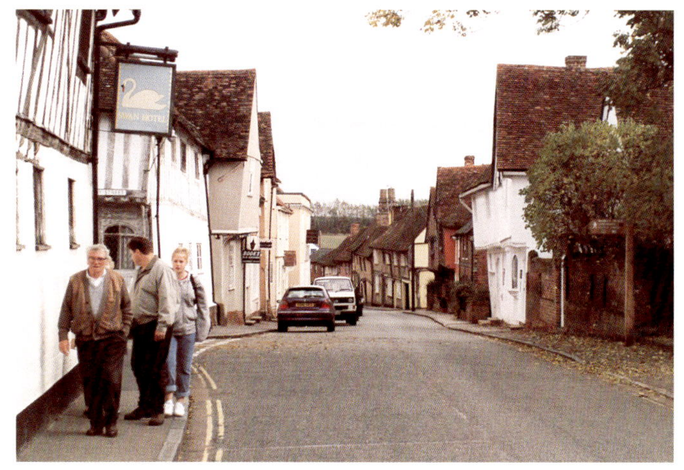

Painting from Photographs

I WOULD like to move on to a subject now which is often the cause of a lot of disappointment to painters and that is painting from photographs. The photograph that you have taken may have been on a beautiful day and a lovely sunny scene but nine times out of ten when you get the developed print back the photograph is often quite dead, flat and boring and this can transfer into your painting if you're not careful. The way to get around this, I've always found, is to introduce more light and depth of shadow and colour into the painting. This brings the whole thing more to life and is far more exciting than the original photograph.

As I've previously said the vast majority of my paintings are done on location but there is no doubt about the fact that photographs have their place in the studio. We have to learn how to paint from these in a more positive manner and remember, we're not photographers. We don't need to have everything in the place that it is in the photograph; we can move a tree slightly to the left or the right or bring it further forward or take it further away. We can alter things slightly and here's and example of what I mean. This is a photograph that I took in the summer of '99 in Lavenham in Suffolk and as you can see from the street in the photograph, it's a very pretty little scene but is, as I've said before, rather flat and boring.

So I introduce more light into the actual painting as you'll see here, with more shadow and more colour. This has brought the whole thing to life more and I add a little more interest into the distance by putting any figures that I was going to have further away down the street.

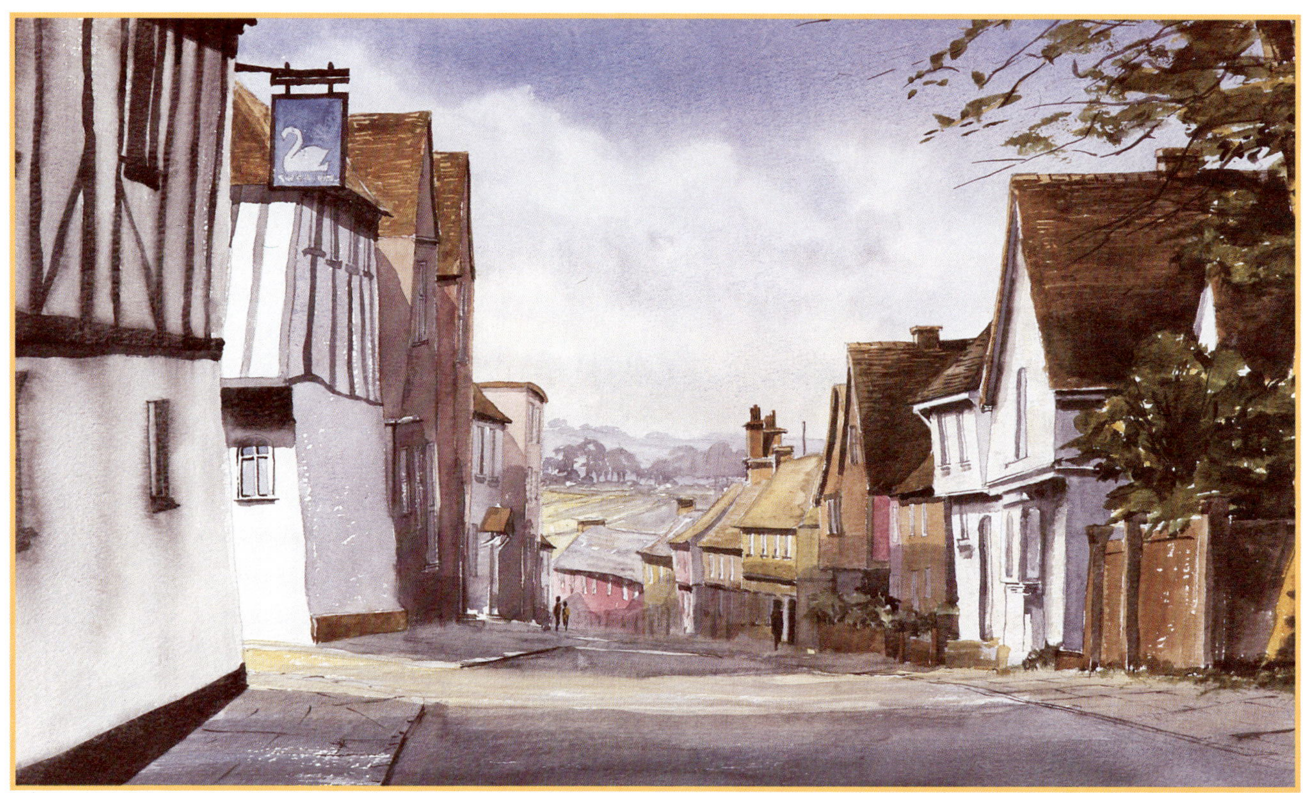

Painting

A Suffolk Lane

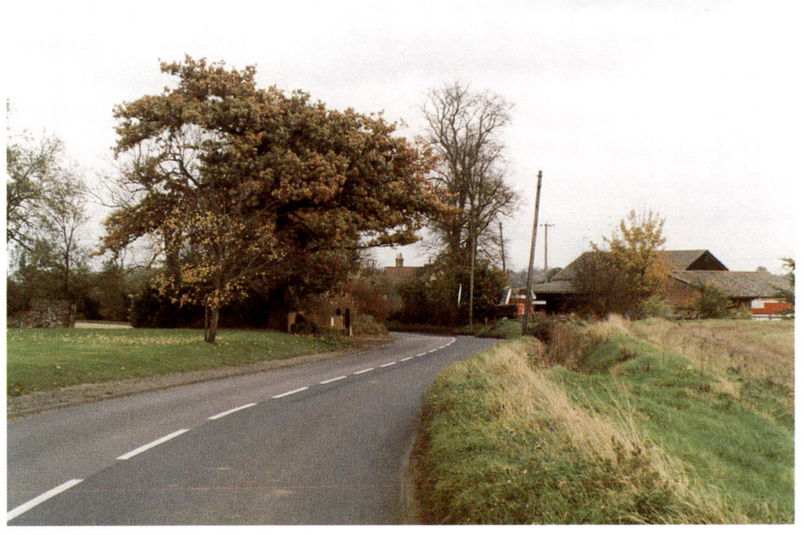

HERE'S another example of a photograph taken in a Suffolk lane on the same day as I took the Lavenham photograph and I'm sure you'll agree it's not the most exciting of photographs and not the most exciting of scenes. But as I'll show you stage by stage, this will make a very pleasing picture with the addition of more shadow, more light and a slightly different perspective of the tree on the left.

Now take a look at the drawing that I've done of this photograph and as you'll see, the tree on the left I've brought further forward and notice at the same time I won't be painting white lines up the centre of the road. I want to make it look more like a track than a tarmaced road. These are the only alterations I've made for the actual drawing. The rest will be done with the colours.

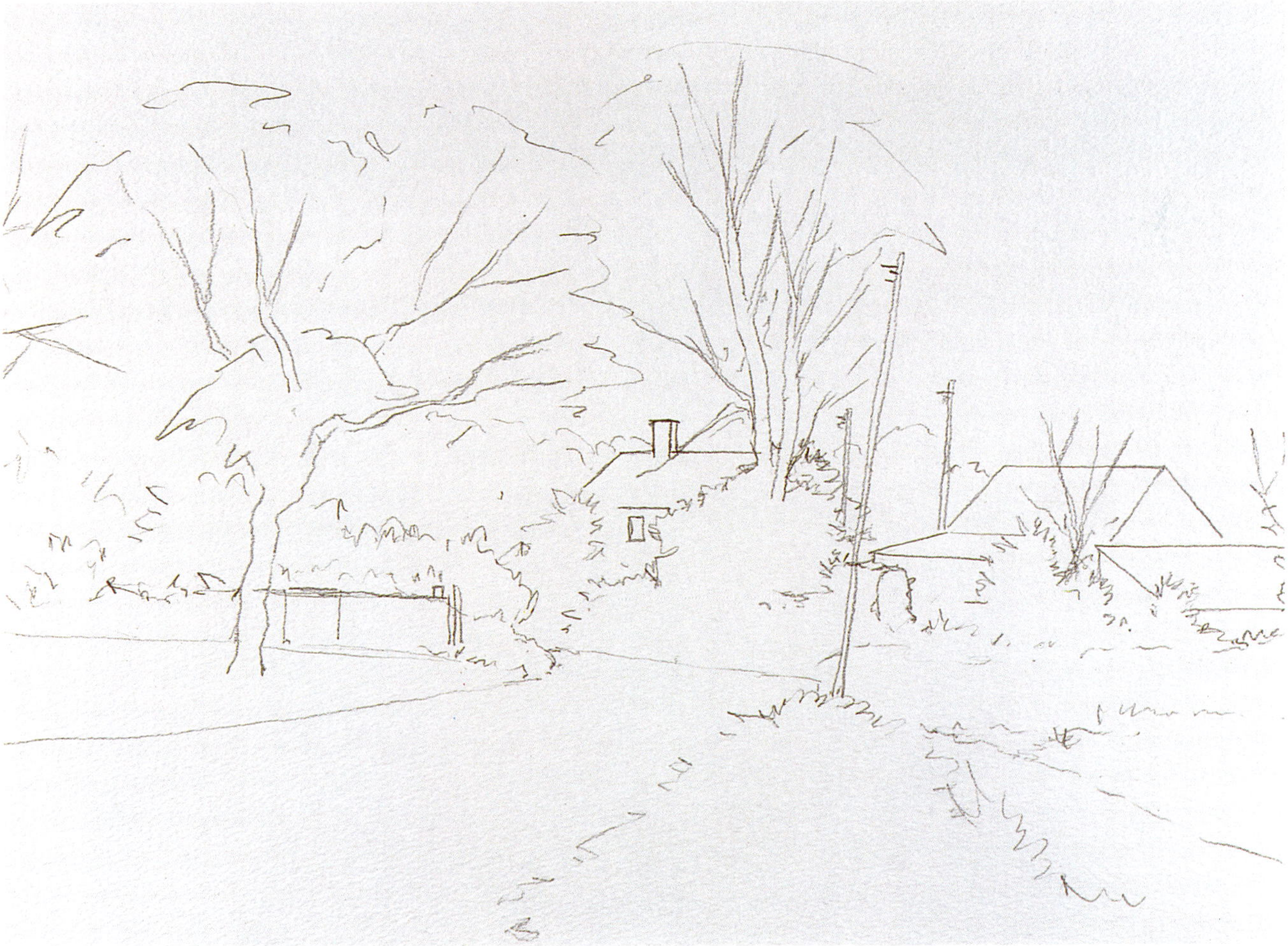

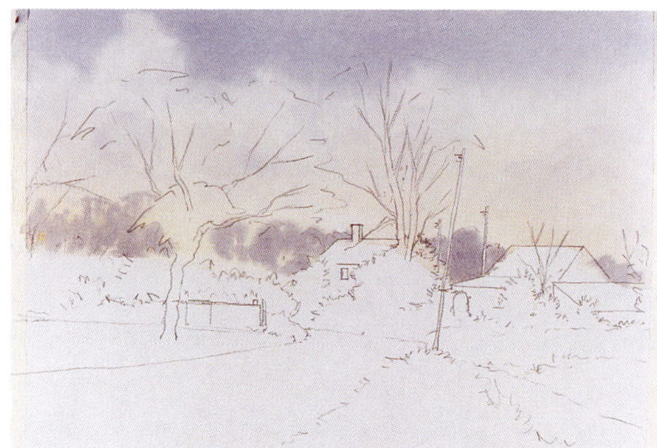

Painting the Sky

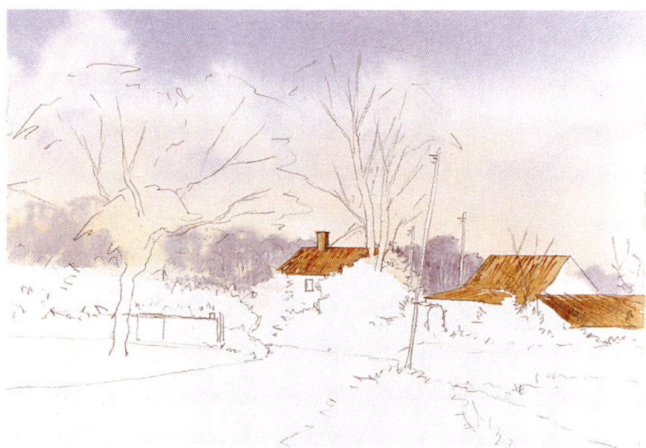

Burnt Sienna for the Roof

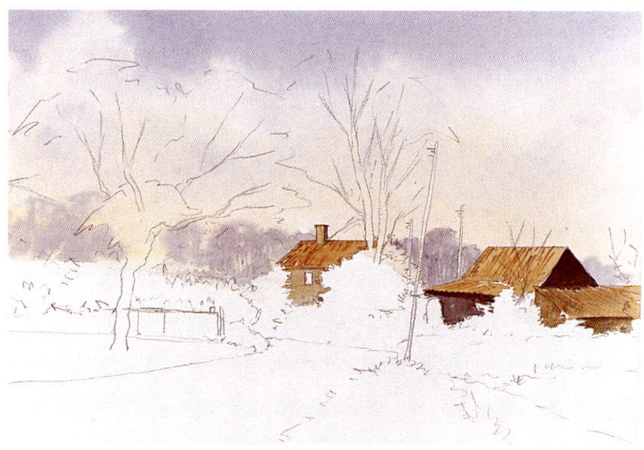

Walls of the Barn

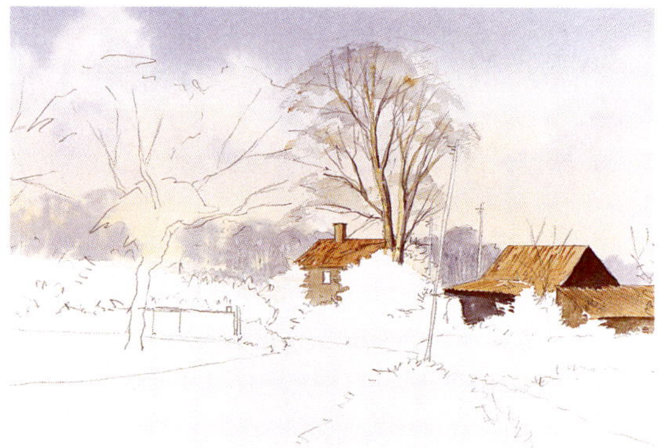

Middle Distance Trees

FOR THE sky in this painting, as you can see, I wet the entire area of the sky first and I go into the bottom areas with a mixture of Yellow Ochre and Alizarin Crimson mixed together with plenty of water. Drop this into the bottom two thirds of the sky.

For the top area I use French Ultramarine Blue with the tiniest touch of Light Red mixed into it just to knock off that bright blueness a little bit. All the way across the top let the colours run down and mingle into each other. I then use my washed and dried out brush and take out some of the clouds in a similar manner to how we've done it in the past. Then into the bottom areas of the clouds I add a mixture of French Ultramarine Blue and Light Red, this time darker and softened it into the cloud areas slightly. Then whilst the sky is still damp I drop in a little French Ultramarine Blue and Light Red, a similar colour to the base of the clouds, into the horizon line of the painting. This will give me the impression of few very distant trees as I look through the trees in the foreground areas.

In this painting I want the light to be coming from the left and in this next photograph I paint the roof of the house which you can see through the trees. This is done with Burnt Sienna, well watered down, for the main roof area and for the chimney standing above it I use Warm Sepia and Burnt Sienna mixed together. Effectively what I've done here is made Burnt Umber. Now you'll notice at this stage that the main part of the chimney is a darker colour to the slither of lighter colour on the left which will be the side that's facing the light. The other roofs I paint with a mixture of Raw Umber with a tiny touch of Burnt Sienna into it. Notice at this stage that I haven't left white areas on these roofs where the trees are going to go in front of them because I want to be able to look through any gaps in the trees and still see the roof at the other side of them.

The walls of the barn, if you look carefully, are black. So I mix French Ultramarine Blue with a touch of Burnt Sienna to go to a really dark colour and make the right hand side slightly darker than the left hand side, so the side facing the light has had a little bit of paint sucked out of it once I've applied it.

Now it's time for those middle distance trees. In this next picture you'll see that I've actually painted the large tree with lots of twigs. I paint this with a mixture of French Ultramarine Blue and Light Red with a touch of Yellow Ochre to the left hand side of the tree so I can capture the light yet again, and I stroke over the top of the tree with dry brush strokes of the same mixture – French Ultramarine Blue and Light Red.

THE TREE directly in front of the barn I give a hint of autumnal foliage with a few strokes of Yellow Ochre and Burnt Sienna mixed in the top. The bushy trees at the base of the middle distance trees I actually paint with a mixture of Hookers Green Dark and Burnt Sienna, just drop those in very liberally and haphazardly to show that they are bushes rather than trees.

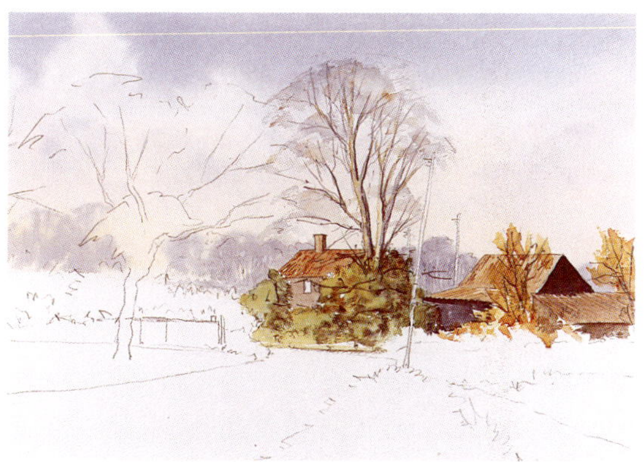

Autumnal Foliage with Yellow Ochre and Burnt Sienna

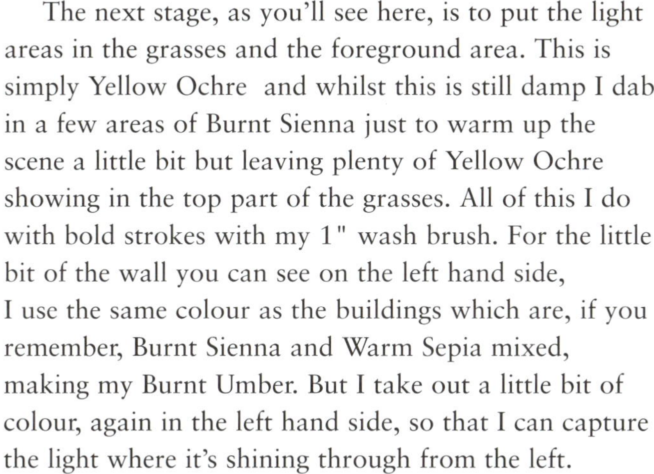

The next stage, as you'll see here, is to put the light areas in the grasses and the foreground area. This is simply Yellow Ochre and whilst this is still damp I dab in a few areas of Burnt Sienna just to warm up the scene a little bit but leaving plenty of Yellow Ochre showing in the top part of the grasses. All of this I do with bold strokes with my 1" wash brush. For the little bit of the wall you can see on the left hand side, I use the same colour as the buildings which are, if you remember, Burnt Sienna and Warm Sepia mixed, making my Burnt Umber. But I take out a little bit of colour, again in the left hand side, so that I can capture the light where it's shining through from the left.

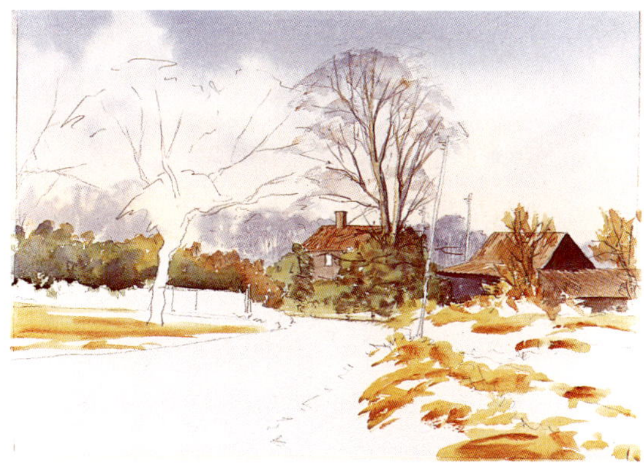

Light areas of the Grasses

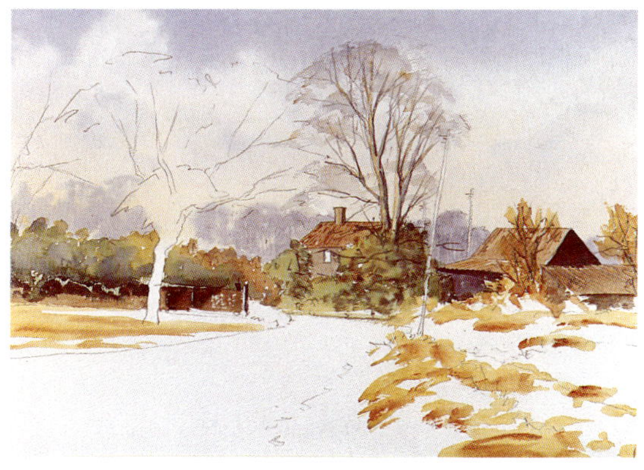

Adding the Wall with Burnt Umber

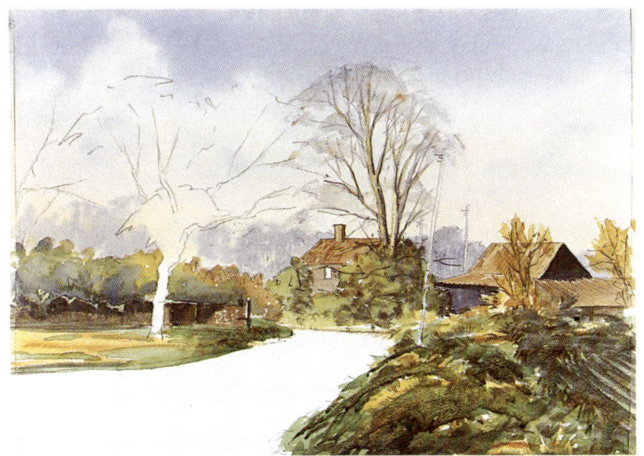

Foreground and Middle Distance Grasses

AS YOU'LL see in the next image I go back to my foreground and middle distance grasses now. Once the Yellow Ochre and Burnt Sienna are dry, with a mixture of Hookers Green Dark and Burnt Sienna I fill in the other areas either side of the yellow bits. Now create the feel of a little bit of undulation in the grasses with the addition of some shadow colour which is French Ultramarine Blue and Burnt Sienna. All this, again, is done with my 1" flat wash brush.

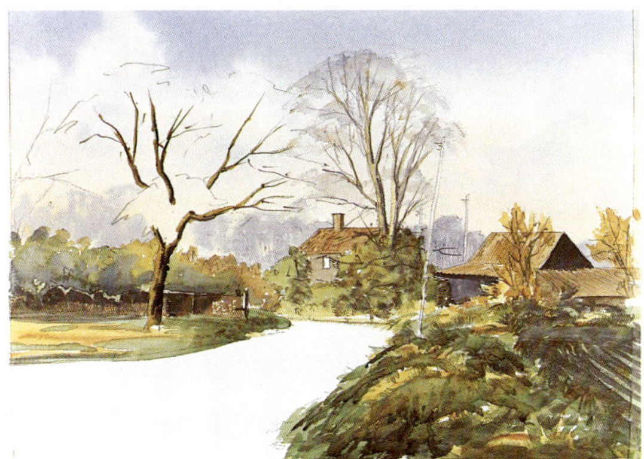

Foreground Tree – Trunk and Twigs

It's time for the large foreground tree now and I start off the main skeleton of the tree with Yellow Ochre on the left hand side all the way up and into the twigs. Then Raw Umber in the central areas finishing off with a mixture of French Ultramarine Blue and Burnt Sienna on the extreme right hand side of the trunk and the twigs. This gives a feeling of the light hitting the left hand side of the tree and being darker on the right hand side with a mid colour in the middle. For the foliage I start off with Yellow Ochre in the top areas of the clumps of foliage and then a mixture of Hookers Green Dark and Burnt Sienna, heavy on the Burnt Sienna because these leaves are just starting to turn and become a slightly autumnal colour. I finish off again with shadow areas in amongst the foliage using my large round brush, just dabbing on a mixture of French Ultramarine Blue and Burnt Sienna.

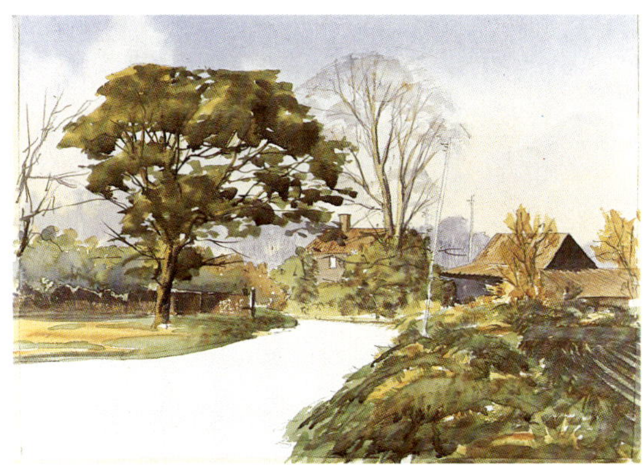

Foreground Tree – Foliage

IN THIS picture you'll see that I've completed the track and the telegraph posts going off into the distance. For the track I use a mixture of French Ultramarine Blue and Light Red, heavy on the red and lighter on the blue so that it gives you a nice warm colour. For the telegraph posts I use a mixture of Warm Sepia with Burnt Sienna, but once I've done my pole I then, with a sharp flat edged brush, take out some of the paint down the left hand side of the pole, again giving the impression that the light is catching the left hand side.

As you see here, the picture is now finished and the finishing touches were the shadows coming from the trees across the track from left to right. In the distance as the road curves round to the left I've put quite a lot of shadows across the road giving the impression that there's a lot of overgrown bits as you turn round the corner. And that's another painting finished, rather more complex but well worth the effort, I'm sure you'll agree. And that just shows that photographs can be made into exciting pictures with the addition of light and atmosphere that we can only create through the colour with our paint brush and an artist's eye.

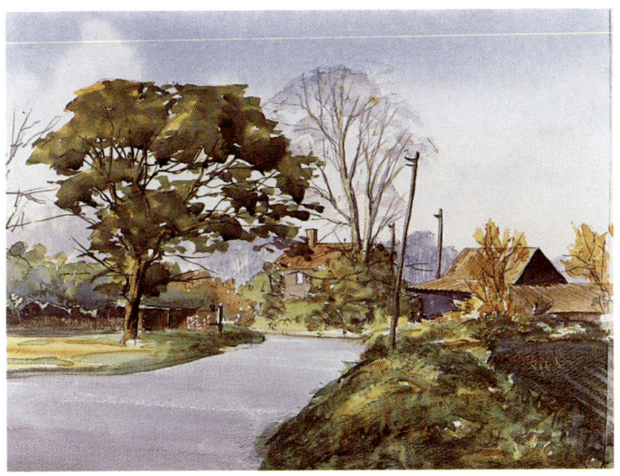

Track and Telegraph Posts

Finishing touches with Shadows

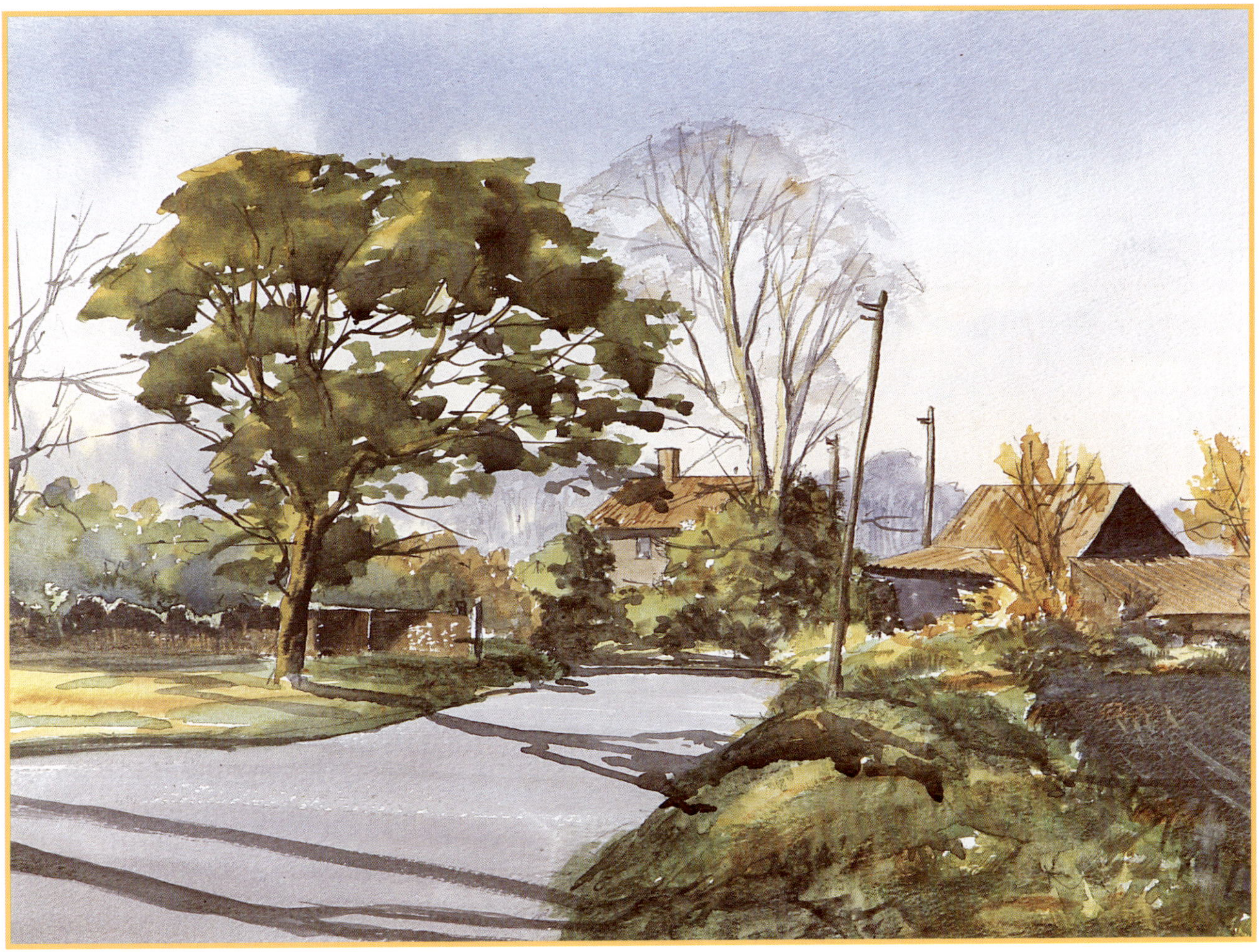

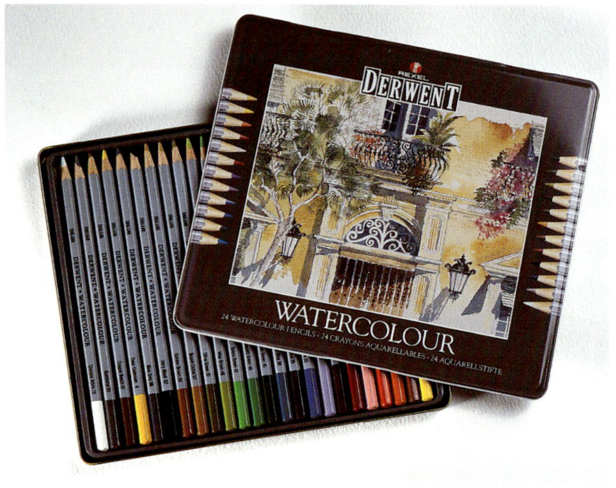

Water Colour Pencils

NOW I'D like to tell you a little bit about something that I consider a really useful tool for sketching out in the field and that is water colour pencils. You can buy a landscape tin of pencils which contains 12 pencils and its all the colours that you're going to need for your average landscape. Literally, all the colours you'll need to take on a sketching expedition is your one tin of pencils, a small jar of water and a medium size paint brush suitable for all occasions. With these pencils you simply draw the subject in the colours that you wish to capture and then just dip your water brush into your water and stroke over the colours. This literally turns it into a mini watercolour painting so that you can really use your sketch book as a reference for colours as well as what the general scene looked like. The water colour pencils that I use are called Derwent and these are exceptionally good water colour pencils with beautiful, vibrant colours. Here's an example.

These trees, path and a bit of grassland are drawn first with my water colour pencils and then, as you'll see in this next picture, this is the result after you've stroked over the whole thing with water.

Unfortunately you can't do a large wash. What you must concentrate on is to do each individual area separately with your brush. For example, stroke the tree first with a little bit of water and then go on to your grasses. And likewise with the distant trees or the sky. You must do each individual area separately otherwise you'll end up with all the colours running into each other. I've always found that these are a very useful piece of kit to keep in my car or in my outdoor clothing pocket. They're always around, so they are useful and suitable for any occasion to make a quick note of any scene that catches my interest which could be later made into a full blown painting.

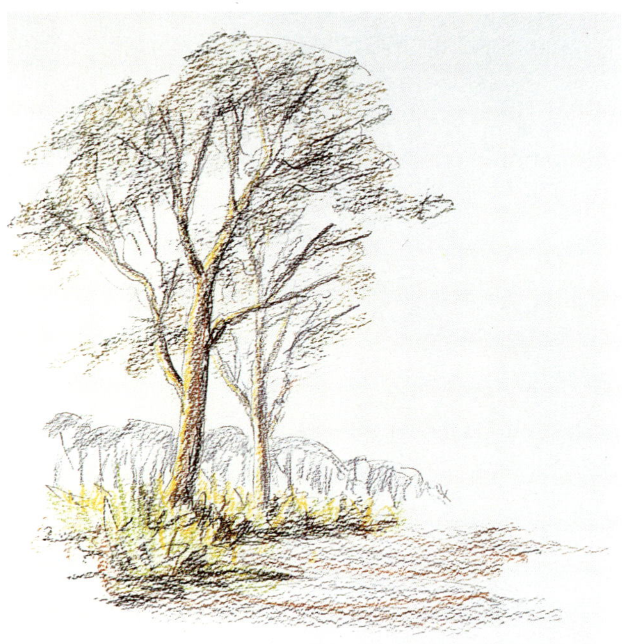

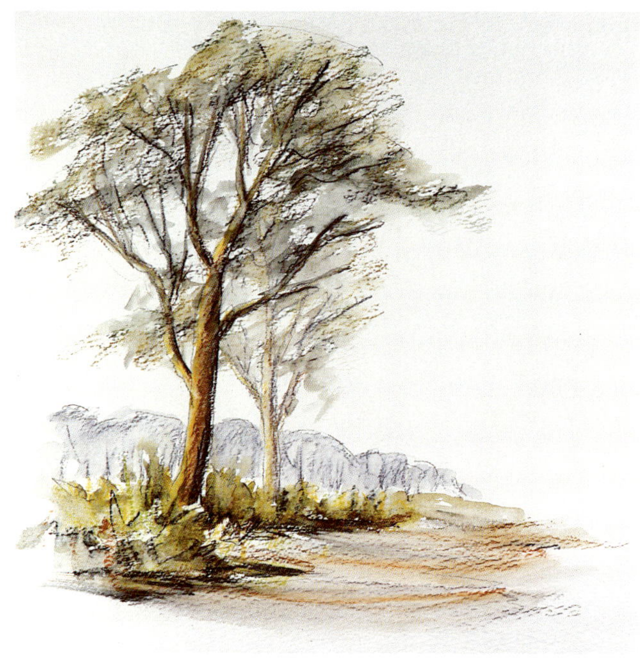

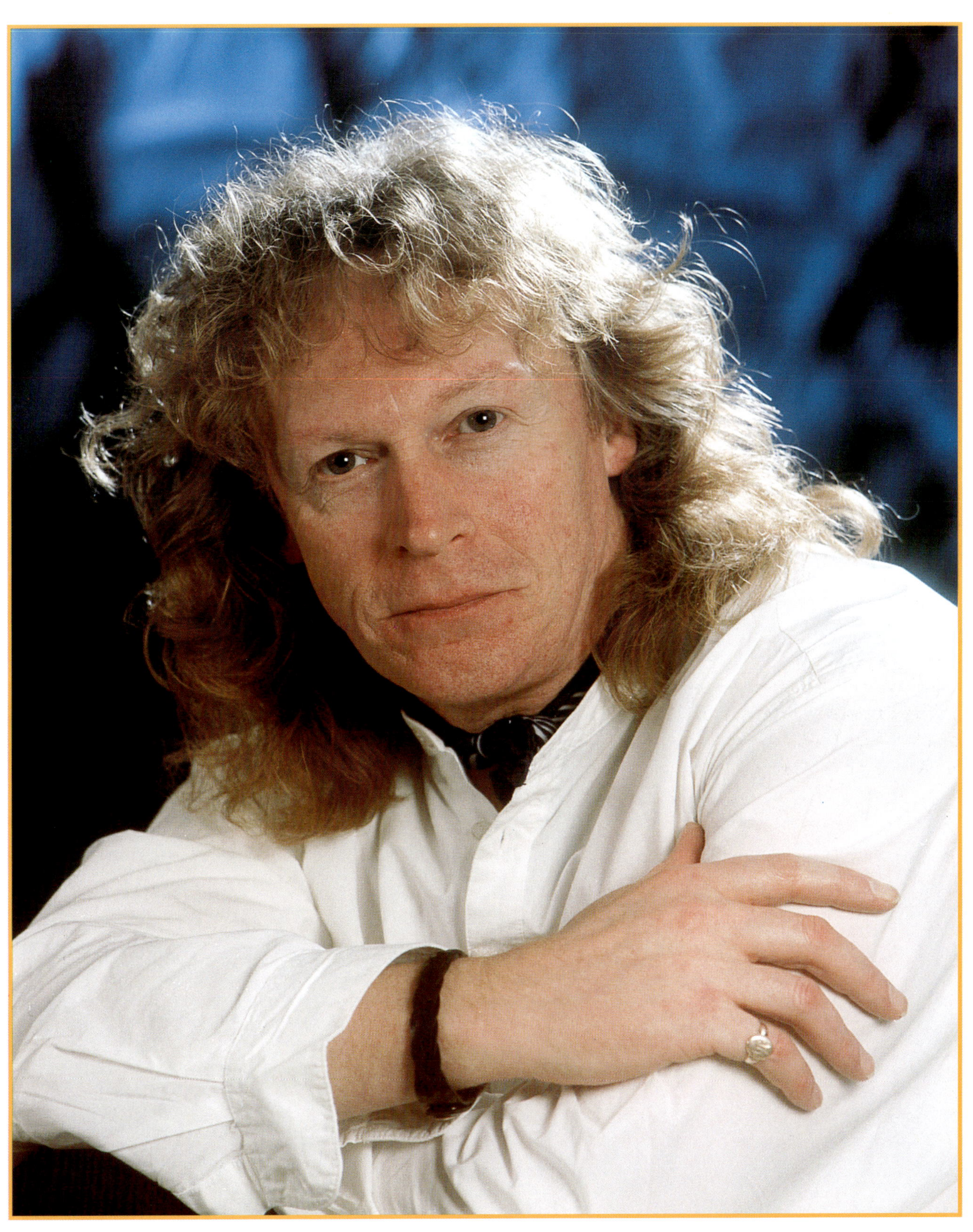

Charles Evans

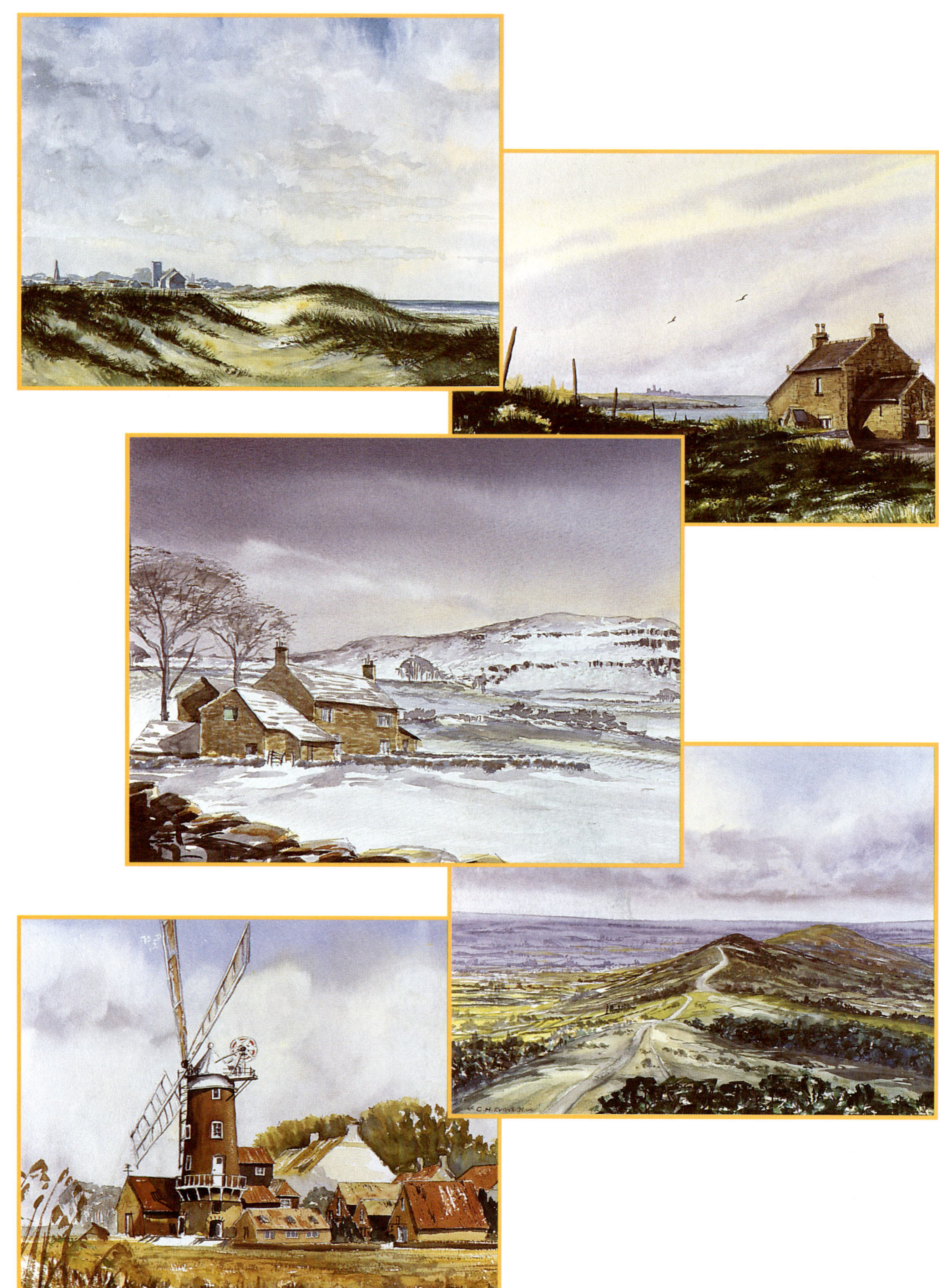

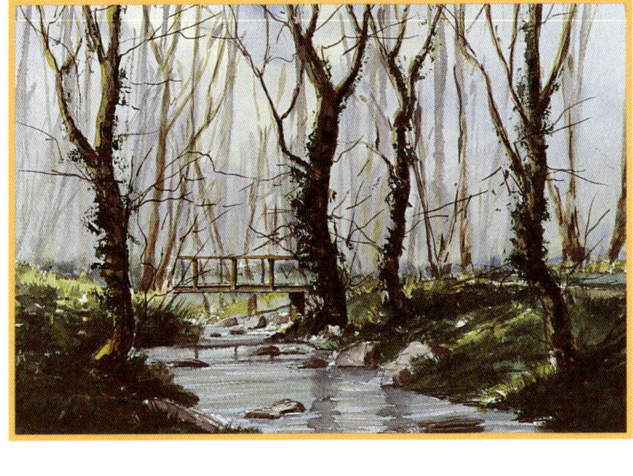

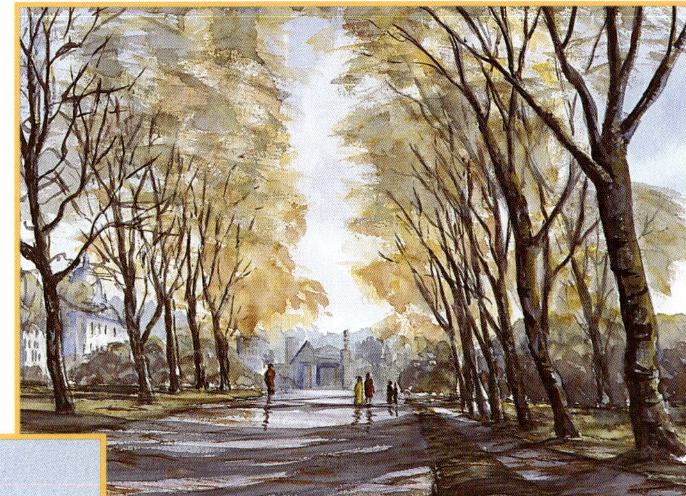

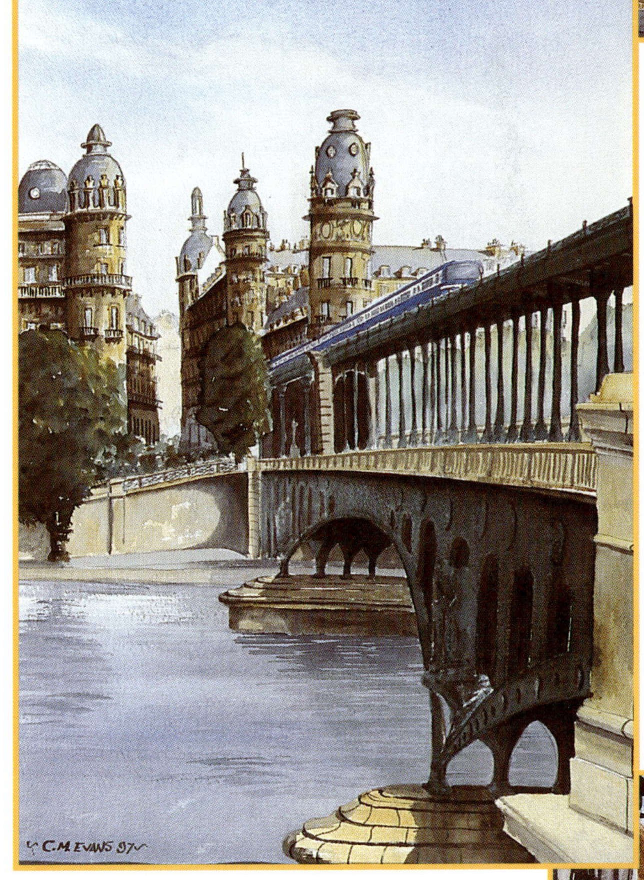
C.M.EVANS 97

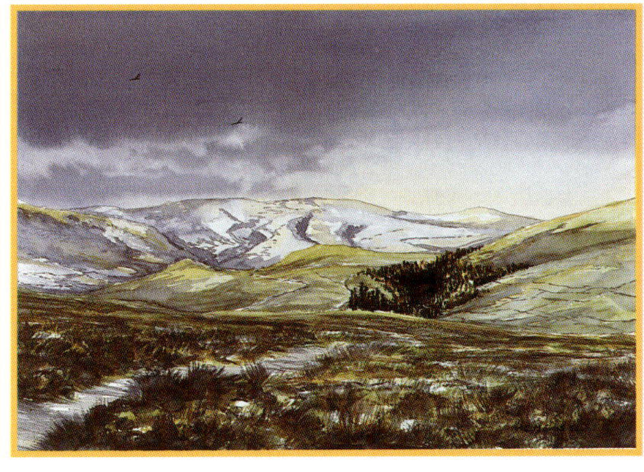

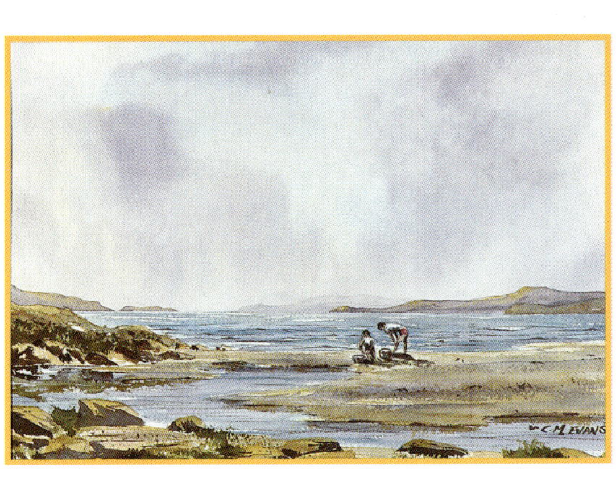
C.M.EVANS

Acknowledgements

AND that's all I want to cover for this book. In the next book I'll be going into more detail and building on some much more complex paintings. It's been a great honour for me to pass on to you some of my knowledge and I can only hope that you've learnt something from reading this book and from doing the paintings stage by stage with me. So for the time being it's, "Goodbye", and I wish you every success with your painting.

Firstly I'd like to thank John Moreels MBE. This book was his original idea. One day at the Ward Graphics Art Show he waved a learn to paint book under my nose and said "I want one of these and I don't want to wait too long for it". Well he's got one and he didn't wait too long.

I'd also like to thank Mark Murray who is my Tyne Tees Television Producer/Director for his very kind comments in the Introduction. It's been great fun working with Mark and over the past couple of years he's become much more than a work colleague, he's become a really great friend. I look forward to many more filming sessions with him on behalf of Tyne Tees Television.

I'd also like to thank Daler-Rowney for their very kind support. Having been a user of Daler-Rowney products for many, many years, as long as I can remember painting, it was a great honour to me to to be actually taken on board by Daler-Rowney to demonstrate their materials and represent them all over the United Kingdom and Europe. I can only reiterate that in my opinion Daler-Rowney painting products are the best quality products available on the market and they've also been around for a very long time. If their products were good enough for the great Turner, then they're certainly good enough for me.

And Yvonne Barnes who without her superb skill at typing at a very rapid pace none of this would have been possible.

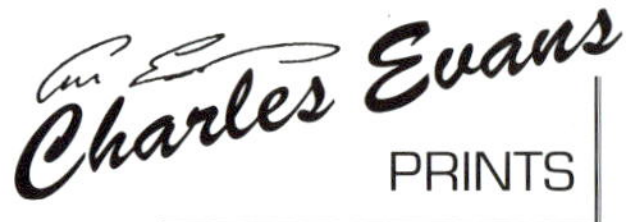

Alnwick Castle, Northumberland

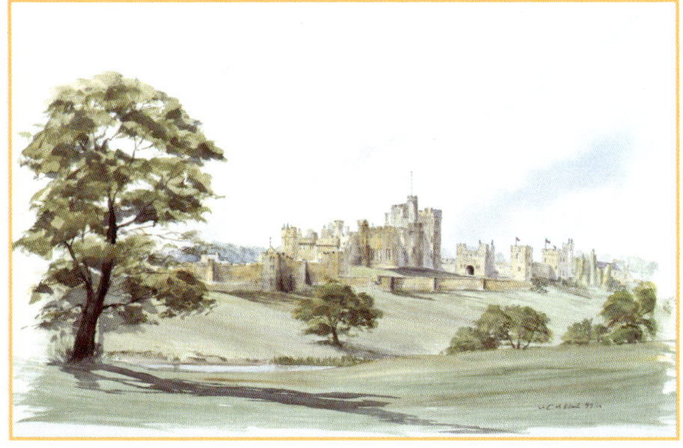

(Size 19½" x 13¾")

Charles painted the original to be auctioned on television to raise funds for Marie Curie Cancer Care. It raised over £600!

You can now obtain a beautiful print of this picture which typifies the beautiful Northumberland Castle and countryside in Charles' relaxing style.

Farm Cottage

by Nathan Summers (Size 20" x 14")

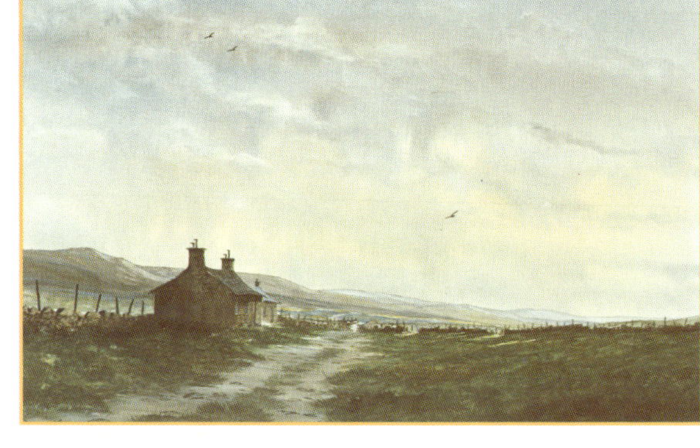

As featured on Yorkshire Television on December 17th, 1998.

A limited Edition of 850 prints, plus 50 Artist's proof copies all numbered and signed by the artist. The finest fade-resistant inks and paper have been selected for this collector's edition.

Yorkshire Television commissioned Charles to paint a large canvas 29ins by 20ins as an important prop in a television drama screened on December 17th 1998. Charles has painted many pictures and won many fans – but his biggest audience was this painting which didn't even bear his name.

The painting showing a scene on the moors above Alnwick is by an artist called Nathan Summers who isn't very famous for the simple reason that he doesn't exist. In fact it was painted by Charles, who lives in Acklington, near Morpeth. The print comes complete with a certificate verifying the fact that the original appeared on television in front of an audience of millions. This is your chance to obtain a limited edition of a unique painting – signed by the actual artist.

The Tyne Tees Television Great North Walk Durham 1999

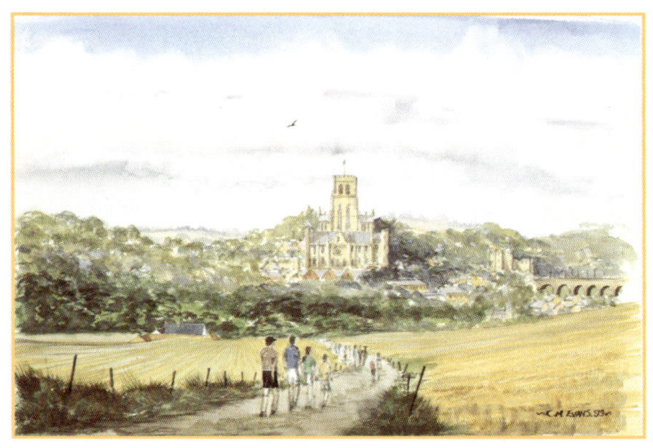

As featured on television. (Size 19½" x 13¾")

Tyne Tees Television commissioned Charles to paint a special unique painting of the 1999 Great North Walk in Durham. Charles has painted many pictures and won many fans with his paintings and prints being sought after throughout the world. Some of the proceeds of this print were donated to cancer charities.

You can obtain a special print issue direct from the publisher, which will enhance any wall at home or office – or as a gift. Available framed or unframed you can order yours now and have it signed by the artist for charity!

If you would like details of any of the above prints, current original paintings available or list of Galleries featuring Charles Evans please contact:

E-mail: charlesevans@theartistshop.co.uk
Call: Charles Evans information (0191) 460 5915 Fax (0191) 460 8540
Write: Charles Evans c/o Ward Philipson Group, Halifax Road, Dunston Industrial Estate, Gateshead, Tyne & Wear NE11 9HW.